AF326516

One Breath

There is no judgment, only love.

By Richard and Laurrana Leigon

No portion of this book was written, outlined, or edited with AI except for a final proofreading pass for typos right before publication.

Richard and Laurrana Leigon

Like Rain books are available at special discounts when purchased in bulk for premiums and sales promotions as well as for fundraising or educational use. Special editions or book excerpts can also be created to specification. For details, contact the publisher at the address below.

Like Rain Publishing
PO Box 13922
Ogden, UT 84412

Printed in the United States of America

First Printing, Hardcover Edition
26 27 28 29 1 2 3 4 5 6 7 8 9 10 11

Contents

Prologue

Richard

I died on October 10, 2022. The Richard that my wife knew took his last breath in the emergency room. Some moments later, a new Richard was born when a beam of light connected me and my wife. In that instant, I gasped air into my body again. I was not the same person afterward. This is the story of what I experienced in the space between those breaths.

Before my death event, I had hopes and beliefs. Afterward, I no longer hoped or believed; *I knew.* This book is about the truths I learned in that other place, including the realization that every step in my life had been orchestrated by the Source of all that is. I had free will at all times, but there were no coincidences. Events in your life are being orchestrated, too.

There are no mistakes along the way, and no judgment—only experiences, only love. All that matters is the universal, unconditional love that surrounds us. You may be weighed down by all that is happening in our world, but if you could see what I saw, your heart would be light. You would understand that a divine plan is at work in all things.

The sections of this book alternate between Laurrana and me because my wife experienced parallel stories. While I was "there," she was grounded here. We have always been two halves of a complementary whole, and when I died, she tethered me back into this world. She gained her own profound insights, and the story would be incomplete without her powerful voice and unique point of view.

Authors' Note

We are proud of our adult children and their families more than we can say. We mention them in this book as they appear directly in the story, but we also respect their privacy. In particular, our daughter and husband are in a line of work where prudence calls for keeping a low public profile. For that reason, we have omitted her name and other details. She knows how much we are in awe of her and how grateful we are for all the support she gives us.

One Breath

Chapter One:

Snapshots of Richard's early life

Richard

My dad was one of many in the construction industry who helped build Las Vegas in the 1950s and '60s. He was an electrician who later rose to prominent leadership positions representing the trade. In those years, Las Vegas had just begun its meteoric rise from a dusty desert town into a dazzling city of air conditioning, slot machines, and 24-7 emptiness. All of that took power, so it was an ideal hometown for an electrician.

One Friday night when I was six or seven, my dad said, "We're getting up early tomorrow and you're coming with me."

We drove downtown to The Mint Hotel, which, at the time, was the tallest on Fremont Street. He let me push the elevator button to the top floor, and we entered the big chandeliered banquet room with its wall of north-facing glass windows. Everybody watched their clocks, and then all of a sudden, I saw a big flash of light followed by this huge mushroom cloud. Then, a seismic shock wave hit the hotel, went through us, and kept going. We had just witnessed an atomic bomb blast from an above-ground test in Nevada.

Sometimes the newspaper printed warnings to avoid drinking milk because radiation comes through in milk and the levels measured too high. In school, we crawled under our desks when the sirens sounded, as if that would protect us from a nuclear blast. My father had served in World War II, and even as the specter of World War II still hung over the grown-ups, America entered a new era, the Cold War.

But kids like me growing up in the '50s didn't think much about war, other than the drills in school. Ours was a childhood of Tonka trucks, metal skates, and hula hoops. My family motored to Disneyland the first year it opened in 1955. Daily entertainment came in the form of a transistor radio and a small, 3-channel TV set. My sister and I watched *Leave it to Beaver* and *American Bandstand*, and the family watched *Lawrence Welk* together on Sundays. Every time the tube burned out, I'd get on my bike and go to Safeway for a replacement tube, which I found next to the slot machines. Yes, Safeway in Las Vegas had slot machines! When I got home, we had to wait for the television to warm up before we could watch it again.

We were a small family, just my mom, dad, sister, and me. My parents gave me a solid foundation in life and modeled a loving and positive relationship. My mom was a housewife whose job was to raise the kids, and when my dad came home, to have his martini and dinner ready. Then, he usually went off to a meeting. He served in leadership roles representing not only union electricians, but he was also a mediator. People were always asking him to be on their board or get involved in their cause because he was so thoughtful, capable, and had a reputation for integrity.

One day in 1960, my dad said, "I'm going to the airport. Come with me." Most fathers of that era wouldn't have considered *inviting* or *asking* their children to do things. They made announcements.

At the time, he was serving in several leadership roles: he was on the Nevada State Democratic Party Central Committee; the state's Democratic Party Convention Chairman; President of the Nevada State AFL-CIO; and simultaneously served as President of the Southern Nevada Central Labor Council. So, when a young senator from Massachusetts needed Nevada's endorsement for his presidential bid, he wanted to meet with my dad.

We walked out onto the tarmac at the executive side of the airport to greet a plane that had just landed. Ground crews rolled up a set of metal stairs, and some entourage members came down first, followed by the senator. He strode over, shook my hand, and crouched down to my eye level. That's how I got to shake the hand of John F. Kennedy.

My dad was not home much because he served on a lot of boards and gave a lot of service to our community. But he only ran for office once as City Commissioner because it opened his eyes to the underbelly of politics. Maybe politics can be unsavory everywhere, but especially in Las Vegas at the time. After losing the race, he said, "Never again. I am not a bought and sold man."

He later met President Reagan, received the "Patriotic Service Award" from the U.S. Treasury Department, and was honored by the Las Vegas Mayor and City Council, which proclaimed "Ralph Leigon Day" on May 22, 1976, after my dad. The governor later honored "Ralph Leigon Day" on April 11, 1986. Today, there is even a little street named Leigon Way after him. He remained active in the Masonic temple throughout life. He was a quiet, kind man of upstanding character, and he gave me big shoes to fill.

I had a strong bond with my mother, Evelyn, and it sometimes drove me crazy when she seemed to read my thoughts. She had a way of knowing what I was feeling even when I didn't.

I never saw my parents argue or fight, and I only remember my dad coming home intoxicated once. They enjoyed spending time together, playing golf, and doing other activities. They were loving but not outwardly affectionate to each other, and the same with us kids. We were loved without being cuddled or told, "I love you."

We had a good home life, yet in retrospect, I craved being part of an extended family because ours was so small. We lived apart from other relatives. It was an era when opportunity-seeking families moved to places like Las Vegas or Southern California, disconnected from previous generations and their traditions. I guess Americans, like my ancestors, had been moving west in search of the dream for a long time. My dad was born in 1917 in a literal covered wagon on the trail as his parents emigrated from Texas to New Mexico.

But I only learned details about our history or extended family as an adult. I knew very little about our indigenous family in North Carolina, although we were proud of the Leigon name with its storied history in Europe.

I just know that for my whole life, I have craved connection. Being with family was one reason I enjoyed spending summers working on my maternal grandparents' farm in St. Joe, Missouri. Aside from bonding with my grandparents, the farm held endless adventures for a boy. When I was little, I collected eggs and fed the chickens with my grandmother. In the afternoon, I helped my grandfather call and feed the pigs. These experiences helped me connect to the natural world, another thread that has always been part of my life.

The year I turned ten, my grandfather got a John Deere tractor for me to drive. I learned to cut, rake, bale and stack hay, and plant wheat, corn, and soybeans. I also learned to disk the fields, harrow the fields, and combine and harvest. My grandmother taught me how to hoe the weeds from a row of corn. My grandparents gifted me the best childhood away from Las Vegas summers. They helped me experience how good it feels to accomplish a job.

Back at home in Las Vegas, going to Griffith Methodist Church was not optional each Sunday. I attended the children's classes in the basement, where cubicles separated the different age groups, and we heard stories from the Bible.

I learned to recite the Lord's Prayer, which I did at my bedside each night. This habit started a lifelong conversation with God, opening a channel so I would listen for the conversations God wanted to have with me. For as long as I can remember, I was listening and seeking.

Then, in my adolescence, something happened that opened my spiritual eyes in a way that I would carry for the rest of my life. When I was about ten, I lay in bed one night and looked up to see a woman standing at the foot of my bed. I froze, petrified. She wasn't an illusion, and she wasn't transparent. Neither of us moved at first, but after a while, she put her hands on my feet, and this made her real. I could feel her hands on my feet.

When she touched me, a warm sense of peace

washed over me. I felt loved and accepted.

Then, she began taking steps backward. With each one, she faded into the night.

I didn't know who she was, and I never told another soul about the experience. I thought about it from time to time as a child, but by my teenage years, I had moved on.

The 60s were a marvelous time for me. The first concert I ever attended as a teenager was The Beach Boys, and in 1964, I got to see The Beatles at the Las Vegas Convention Center. We believed our generation would change the world, and that we were part of something special—a collective "we," not just "me." Music played a big part in that, and it was phenomenal. Appreciating music remains a big part of my life.

My formative years were marked by events like the Civil Rights movement, the assassinations of Martin Luther King Jr. and Robert Kennedy, the Kent State Massacre, and the Vietnam War. I especially remember the day John F. Kennedy was killed. It didn't seem possible that the man I had met with my dad that day at the airport could be dead. We were all in shock, just heartbroken.

The world was changing fast, and my generation both absorbed and created tremendous upheaval. Much of humanity seemed ready to let go of beliefs that only served some people. Other people fought to keep things the same. I believed we were ready for a new way.

I had grown up going to church, but by that time in my life, the rigid constraints of religion seemed far too limiting to me, and I became disillusioned. I believed that religion should be self-empowering so people could have a stronger relationship to God, not just dictate rules that seemed to separate church members from the "sinners." It was a real problem for me when I saw churches doing more to put people into boxes rather than encouraging them to grow. They did more to divide people than bring them together, so I stopped going.

After graduating from high school, I couldn't get out of Las Vegas fast enough. I just could never imagine myself staying in the same town where I was born. The world seemed bigger than that.

My dad offered me a tremendous gift by helping me get admitted to the U.S. Naval Academy in Annapolis. He had gone to a lot of effort to help get me into such a prestigious program, and I knew how much it meant to him. I didn't want to be ungrateful. He had served in the Navy during the war (although he never talked about it), and he never had such an opportunity handed to him. We both knew it would write my ticket for the future. It ate me up inside to disappoint my dad.

But something else inside called to me. I felt a pull toward spiritual matters in a way that my practical dad would never quite understand. Yes, he saw that our family attended church, and he was a man of irreproachable integrity, a good man. But he stayed grounded in practical matters of this life.

How could I tell him I wanted to reject his gift? I had no idea where my heart might lead, but times were changing, and I felt part of it. I was choosing the hippie scene instead of a crew cut.

I gave him the bad news and ultimately ended up at college in California.

The first year after I left for school, I remember my mom calling before I returned for Christmas and saying, "There's only one thing I really, truly want for Christmas. Would you please cut your hair?" I had a close relationship with my mom and wanted to please her, but I couldn't bring myself to cut my hair.

Snapshots of Laurrana's early life

Laurrana

I grew up in Marin County, a suburb just north of San Francisco and the Golden Gate Bridge, in a nice, family-oriented community. My mother, Maryann, was the most strong-willed person I ever met, a devoted Catholic who recited the rosary twice a day without fail. She believed in miracles, and I remember her telling me, "Your spirituality is your most important thing in your life, no matter what else happens."

I was the eldest, and when I turned six, my mother contracted polio and spent a year in the hospital. My dear father, Jack, had little choice but to farm each of us children out to live with different relatives while he worked two jobs to pay the medical bills. I went with my dad's sister and her husband. I felt terribly homesick and told my dad that I didn't want to be there anymore. I have never forgotten how loved I felt when he did not question my request. He listened and brought me home with him right away. This created a tremendous hardship for him to arrange four or five different places for me to be throughout the day while he worked, but he did it for me.

One evening, I was supposed to be asleep in bed, but I heard a noise, crept downstairs, and looked into the kitchen. From a distance, I peered at my dad, slumped at the table with his head in his hands, sobbing. I felt so sorry for him, but I couldn't let him know I saw him. The next morning, he was in the kitchen again, cheerfully making me breakfast, but now I understood the sorrow he carried. I still ache inside when I think of it.

He was twenty-eight when that happened.

None of us knew whether our mother would come home. She eventually did, but the medical bills avalanched our family. She had been a dancer and a tennis player, and she would never walk again. I learned to take care of her and help her navigate life from a wheelchair from that time forward.

My parents clung to each other after polio and had a solid, loving relationship. They were a product of their time and not overtly affectionate, but loyal and close to each other. They might express their emotions about any given topic to us, but children were not to question what they thought or felt.

Both of my parents were people of outstanding integrity and great character. They persevered through their challenges with grace and dignity. I admired their ability to give back to others even amidst their own difficulties. Despite the challenges we faced as a family, my parents prioritized education. They expected me to go to college and supported me in doing so. That remains one of the greatest gifts they ever gave me.

My family's relationship to the Catholic Church became mixed after my mother contracted polio. My father remained active, but his relationship cooled when the Church did not step forward to help more during this time. My mother had given so much of herself to the Church, joining a convent before marrying and organizing many fundraisers for others. But when we hit hard times, they said we were on our own. Still, my mother's faith and her activity in the Church remained stalwart throughout her life.

I cherished a close relationship with my maternal grandmother and saw how heartbroken she was that her daughter would never walk again. In tribulation, my mother and grandmother both clung to their Catholic faith, but the two women went about religion in different ways. At times, my mother didn't like it when I spent time at my grandmother's home because of the influences or ideas I might pick up there.

My mother was rigidly connected to the church's rules, whereas her mother, Ursula, had seen a lot more of the world and practiced a more fluid form of religion. Ursie, as loved ones called her, would take me to the Christian Science Library to read. I remember her repeating affirmations aloud, visualizing ideas she had for abundance. She believed in making the invisible visible. With very few resources, she found a way to create the home, lifestyle, and relationships she desired. She also took me down to Haight Street, where we fed the homeless. She had gay friends, but my mother treated it like a cold you might catch if you were exposed. She was a lot of fun to be around, too.

My paternal grandmother, Aznive, also had a profound impact on who I grew up to be. She was raised in the Armenian Orthodox Church, and those traditions were interwoven throughout her life. Her entire family, including her first husband, was wiped out in the mass Armenian genocide, and she witnessed many of them being killed. An estimated 1.5 million Armenians were murdered or displaced in the early twentieth century by the Ottoman (Turkish) Empire in a state-planned genocide of this Christian minority group.

My grandmother escaped by hiding in a cellar for weeks, came to America at age fifteen with a soldier who would soon become my grandfather, and became the most fearless person I have ever met.

Shortly after she arrived in the United States in 1915, she gave an interview for a newspaper about the genocide, and that article was reprinted in papers around the country. After that, she did not talk about that horrific experience because she didn't want other people to bear that burden. She just split that part of herself off. Yet, she had strong spiritual gifts going back to the old traditions, including reading Turkish coffee grounds. She saw those same traits in me and encouraged me to develop them. I credit a lot of my intuition to her, partly because she encouraged me to flex the muscle to make it strong.

My mother would have been concerned about what I learned from my grandmother because her gifts were not sanctioned by the Catholic Church. In centuries past, that sort of thing got witches burned at the stake. But I gravitated there anyway. Something inside told me how important it was to learn all I could from this great woman and to nurture this side of myself.

Ultimately, I recognize that differences in all relationships are part of life, and differences within my family have been just as much a blessing as other gifts they generously gave. In the end, it's all a gift. I am in debt to my parents and grandparents for their devotion, love, and support in helping me become the person I am today.

The first time my life was spared

Richard

In the fall of 1968, my parents supported my going to the University of Nevada, Reno, for my freshman year. I did fine academically, but didn't feel at home there. I soon learned that there are entrenched rivalries between Reno and Las Vegas, and they really don't like kids from Las Vegas there. So, for my sophomore year, I decided to transfer to Orange Coast College in Costa Mesa, California.

I began taking classes in a new field called humanistic psychology, distinguished from clinical psychology at the time. It emphasized looking at people's development holistically, not just what was going on in the mind. The field emphasized self-awareness and personal growth. I found it absolutely fascinating, and it just clicked with me. I finished my associate's degree there. Meanwhile, my roommate Steve taught me how to surf, repair surfboards, and shape and fiberglass them.

I went home for the summer of 1969. By then, I was a long-blonde-haired hippie, and I bought myself a Triumph Bonneville motorcycle. It wasn't a stock model, more like an easy-rider type. Anyway, I had a friend, Louie, who lived in Newport Beach, California, and we planned a trip up the Pacific Coast Highway. So, I hopped on my bike at dawn to make it across the Mojave Desert before the day's heat.

We set off for Big Sur, and I soon learned the trip would take longer than planned because he had to call his new girlfriend every time he saw a pay phone.

It was just one of those things.

Spectacular scenery flanked us on both sides, with cliffs and crashing waves hundreds of feet down. At one point, Louie had driven out in front of me, and I noticed that we passed a turnout with a pay phone overlooking the cliffs. It would be a prime spot to stop and check out the ocean.

So I sped up and told him that we'd just passed a phone booth and then flipped around to double back. He lagged somewhere behind when I approached the turnout. It was a nice, flat, packed-dirt area. I slowed down and checked my speed, then swore under my breath. The turnout wasn't as long as I thought. I might not stop the bike in time, and remember thinking, *This isn't going to work!*

I put my feet on the ground and had already hit the clutch when I pulled hard on the rear brake. This made the bike want to jerk around. I was losing control fast.

The front of the bike nosed over the cliff's edge, and the foot peg caught a shrub. My hands gripped the bars, and I desperately tried to figure out how to pull it back over the edge without my feet slipping out from under me, hurtling me and the bike hundreds of feet below into the rocky surf.

As the front tottered over the edge, I felt

something grab the back of the bike and pull it back onto the ground. Louie was still nowhere in sight.

I don't know what else to say except that it felt like a hand came out of thin air and stopped that bike from going over the edge.

A few moments later, Louie showed up and pulled me and the bike back from the brink. We continued our ride, and I couldn't stop thinking about the hand. It would stick with me as one of the most profound experiences of my life.

Chapter Two: Twin Flames

A shared spiritual path

Richard

For my upper-division college work, I went on to Sonoma State University (S.S.U.) in Rohnert Park, California. The emerging field of humanistic psychology lit me up, and I was eager to finish my degree.

My mentor and personal faculty advisor was Dr. Eleanor Criswell Hanna, the Founding Director of the Human Psychology Institute.

Her opening statement to students was, "We are humanistic and holistic by nature of our approach. We honor you for who you are and where you are at this moment in time. Love is powerful, as well as the subconscious mind."

During my time at S.S.U., she headed up the psychology department. Eleanor was also a Somatic Yoga instructor. From her, I learned the practice of yoga and breathing techniques to bring about a higher state of consciousness. This is where spiritual alignment occurs.

I graduated, and a bunch of us guys went on summer adventures while one friend, Mike Atchison, stayed and rented a house in the small, quaint town of Kenwood. As the summer of '72 drew to an end, we returned and descended upon Mike's house in Kenwood.

The Chinese owner of the house lived in San Francisco and, unannounced, drove up to Kenwood to check in on his rental. Needless to say, he was shocked to find four guys living in a house he had rented to one.

He became rather excited and, yelling in Mandarin, kicked us all out except for Mike. So, I jumped in my blue Ford Econoline, Andy jumped in his Helm's Bakery truck, and Doug rode along as we drove away looking for a place to hang our hats. We ended up circling our wagons pioneer-style on this big field across the street in front of campus. We decided to save on rent and just stay there in our vans.

I started my master's program while still living out of my van. The guys called me the "Sears Roebuck hippie" because I was always so clean, regularly going to the laundromat and folding my clothes. I had a friend named Janet (not a girlfriend) who let me shower at her place. One day, I went to Janet's apartment to shower, and she pointed across the way and said, "You see that girl over there? She really likes you."

And I was like, Hmm, okay. I'll have to take a second look.

Then, unbeknownst to me, Janet goes to this girl and says, "You know that guy who showers at my place? We're not together, and he told me he really likes you."

Not long after that, I got a job on Fridays in the "Dungeons of Darwin," Darwin being the science building. In the basement, they set up tables for collating the school newspaper. It didn't pay a lot, but when you're living out of your van, anything helps. As fate would have it, Laurrana also got a job down there, and that's how it started. We talked while preparing papers, and soon discovered how much we enjoyed each other's company.

From that time forward, we have always been together. We started as best friends and bonded in what has felt like something deeper than just finding someone and falling in love.

Laurrana has always had the same knack my mother had for knowing what I am feeling before I do.

I remember a time early in our relationship, I got cranky, and she told me, "You need to go away."

Her comment puzzled me, and I said, "I don't know what you mean."

She said, "You need to go into your cave and process." She could see what I needed when I was too far into the forest to see it. It's funny because by the time I become cognizant that I need to work through something, I probably have a handle on it. It's that time in the middle when she can see what I can't.

I don't know how she does it, but Laurrana can feel five or six different things and still be present at the same time, absolutely, totally present. For me, simultaneously processing five or six different things would be completely confusing.

It escapes me now who first observed that she and I are not so much soul mates, but twin flames. I think that is the best description. You can talk to either of us, and you are kind of talking to the same person. We just happen to be two different hearts beating.

26

Some people believe you can have more than one soulmate in your life, but twin flames are different. Twin flames are like two halves of a whole, two beings who share a common purpose and journey. When twin flames come together, it feels like destiny because they are both compatible and are also called on a shared mission. They will travel that journey together throughout this life.

Janet is still a very dear friend of ours, and we call her *The Matchmaker* to this day.

While in the first year of my master's program, I learned that you had to be employed in the field to continue. There were too many students looking, and too few jobs out in the community. So, that was the end of my master's program. The C. G. Jung Institute Zurich recruited me, but my parents were not about to send me to Switzerland.

Instead, someone I knew ended up at a Kundalini yoga ashram in Oahu, and my intuition whispered that I should check it out, too. I was ready to escape the California scene.

It was a nourishing community where we lived the life of yogis. We got up before sunrise, did two-hour meditations, took cold showers, and only ate healthy food. No drugs or alcohol. Oh, and they required not cutting your hair, which they believed is related to your life force. So, I fit right in.

Laurrana followed as soon as she could wrap up her bachelor's degree. We married there in 1975 and wanted to start a family right away, so our daughter was born in Hawaii. She was blonde, beautiful, and perfect.

To keep ourselves in groceries, we took on odd jobs, and both of us drove a taxi for a while. We also taught yoga at community rec centers.

We found out that it's hard to get a job with a psychology degree unless you want to work for the Department of Social Services, and I had a sense of what that path would look like. There are more cases than there are minutes in a day, and you may not be helping anybody. So, to support our little family, I returned to my roots. I started my training to become an electrician. We were so happy. *So happy.*

A statue of Mary

Richard

After the electrician jobs dried up in Hawaii, we moved to California to follow jobsite opportunities. By this time, our family was complete with a beautiful daughter and son. He greeted us with red hair and freckles, a nod to my Irish ancestral line.

One day, we were out running some errands, and I had a distinct impression that I should find a Catholic bookstore.

I asked Laurrana, "Do you know where there is a Catholic bookstore? I feel like I need to go to one for some reason."

She took me there without either of us knowing why. We ambled around the store until I spotted a ceramic statue of Mother Mary. The moment my eyes landed on her, I flashed back in full, vivid detail to the woman at the foot of my bed when I was a child. *This was her.* I brought that figurine home and, since then, have placed a few more statues and photos of Mother Mary around our home.

It has since occurred to me to feel grateful that my connection with Mother Mary feels pure without the constraints of dogma. Since I grew up in a Christian faith that did not have a lot of symbolism wrapped up in Mary, there were no expectations about what she should be. I've just felt a love toward her like I might for a mother. My relationship with her is personal and close. It echoes the feelings I have toward my own mother.

I once spoke with a spiritual medium and asked who the woman had been at the foot of my bed, and she responded, "That was Mary. The act of touching your feet was to ensure your heart would stay open in this life."

Mary would remain part of my spirituality throughout my life, but I couldn't begin to imagine the crucial role she would play later.

Chapter Three: Growth

The twin flame journey isn't easy

Laurrana

Some people have written that twin flame relationships can be tumultuous. Somebody we met at a Whole Life Expo once observed that we each carry a lot of voltage in our personalities, and he wondered how the two of us could exist under one roof without blowing up the house.

The truth is, though, that our relationship has not been tumultuous because we are so compatible and supportive of one another.

Our difficulties have come in navigating the trials that life has thrown at us. Our parents did not approve of the unconventional spiritual path we chose. One example is that my mother was especially troubled that I left the Catholic Church, concerned that her granddaughter would not be baptized.

One time when my mother visited, she brought our two-year-old daughter into the kitchen sink and baptized her. There was no waiting for a priest or worrying about protocol. She just took it into her own two hands to make sure her granddaughter had this blessing to bring protection of the church for the rest of her life. And do you know what? To this day, our daughter has a strong affinity with the Catholic church. For me, Catholicism is a part of my cultural and traditional roots and less of a religious identity.

Finding Sharon's grave

Laurrana

In 1981, we were devastated when Richard's mother died suddenly from a brain aneurysm. His father went to sleep, and when he awoke, she had passed away. It came as a terrible blow, and so of course, we drove to Las Vegas to be there during that time and for the funeral.

After her graveside service, I felt drawn to another part of the cemetery, and I walked straight to the headstone of Sharon Leigon, who died as an infant.

"Is this your baby sister?"

Richard followed me, astonished by what had just happened. "I have never seen this. I didn't even know where her grave was."

Richard had hardly mentioned that he had another sister. His parents never spoke of her while he was growing up, and he was almost an adult before he learned about her. I had only known that she lived a very short life and died of sudden infant death syndrome. But I walked straight there.

That was not the first or last time I found someone in a cemetery like that or have been flooded with emotions.

As I contemplated her life, I felt an inexplicable, visceral swell of connectedness to this little soul whose life on earth ended not long before mine began. She and I had Richard in common. I have always felt connected to Richard's family, and this uncanny experience deepened that bond even more.

Mouthing off to The Voice

Richard

I was just thirty-eight years old when my mom passed, and I was devastated. I had expected her to outlive my father. This was my first loss of life, and this was my mom. Now there was only me, my father, and sister. I took it hard; my grief ran deep, and I could not work for two or three weeks.

Just before dusk one evening, I lay on my back in our master bedroom, grieving the loss of my mom. As golden light filtered through the curtains, I looked up, and suddenly, standing at the foot of my bed, clear as day, was my mother.

Her mouth didn't move, but I heard her voice in my mind say, *You're going to be alright.*

Startled and confused, I whispered, *What?*

Then my mom said, "You're going to get through this, and you will be okay."

Her words washed over me like the warm embrace of her love. Then she faded, just like Mother Mary had done at the foot of my bed all those years ago when I was a boy.

At the time my mother appeared to me, I thought she meant I would get through my grief, but

I couldn't comprehend then that my struggles were just beginning. If I had known we were about to hit the lowest point in our lives thus far, I might have had more of a sense of foreboding rather than comfort.

After my mother's death, two more life-altering events would soon devastate us. People say that things have a way of hitting in threes, and that's what happened to me.

The second event was that, less than a year after my mom's passing, my business partner drained all the accounts and disappeared with my name on the line for our debts.

I lost my electrical contracting business, and it felt like I had been whacked with a two-by-four. I got angry.

By this point in my adulthood, I had come to refer to the divine presence in my life as "The Voice," because it felt like it had been in conversation with me throughout my life. It whispered to me in quiet ways, through inspiration, and sometimes in clear words that came to my mind in a flash. I often spoke my questions and ideas back, whether in my mind, or sometimes aloud through prayer. But at this low point, my words were not very meek. I was upset—even sarcastic—and I mouthed off.

I distinctly remember saying to The Voice,

"Come on, you can do better than that."

Things got worse. When my mother died, it felt like I had been hit with a two-by-four. The second event in our lives—losing the business—had escalated the emotional beating I was taking. That felt like I had been hit by a telephone pole. Yet, I was still standing.

I said to The Voice, "Okay, now what do you have to say?"

I was wondering what I had done to have my life go to hell. I thought I had been standing on firm ground. My spiritual discipline was strong, I was focused, and was feeling my oats.

Then, a third event happened, and I wouldn't be standing by the end of it. We had remained part of an ashram when we moved to California, and the Yoga leader there betrayed us in a life-altering way. He turned out to be a classic fraud whose charisma had gained him a cult following.

When that happened, it yanked the rug from under my feet with such force that it flattened me. I was stronger than a two-by-four and stronger than a telephone pole. I was not stronger than the rug.

I do not recommend mouthing off to The Voice. It was my darkest hour, and it flattened me. I felt completely abandoned.

And then something happened. I began to

hear The Voice speaking to me in a more direct way. It had been years since I'd heard it, and now it was part of my life again. It let me know when I needed to hear something, know something, or change something.

I learned another valuable lesson, too. These three experiences were among a few that taught us the hard way that sometimes, even when you go along with good intentions, others may not have your best interests at heart. We learned why a home needs fences, gates, doors, and locks. Give-give people attract take-take people.

One day during that time, I remember saying to myself, "I'm stranded in the middle of nothing and everything."

That's when I heard instructions in my head: Get in the car and go to the bookstore in Carmel Valley.

Once I got there, I felt guided toward a certain aisle where a book quite literally fell off the shelf. It was written by Solara and came with a cassette tape. One powerful segment changed my whole perspective: "Be the star that you are."

That tape was exactly what I needed to hear. *Bam!* I was on my way again.

At the end of that period of our lives, we had been emptied of our jobs, home, friends, and our religious community. It was our lowest point, and we decided it was time for a fresh start. Our little family left for Colorado—Laurrana, our two adolescent children, and I. It's where The Voice whispered that we should go.

The last time

Laurrana

Not long before we left California, I had felt guided toward the field of hospice work. It would become a thirty-year career primarily as a hospice bereavement and comfort care coordinator. My undergraduate program in sociology prepared me for the social services, while my intuitive gifts were more than academic.

I fell into hospice work in the early 1980s when I got hired to work as an activity director for three long-term assisted-living facilities. After just a few days on the job, the facility owner visited and observed me at work. He remarked on how patients and their families were listening to what I had to say and were calm and peaceful as a result. It came naturally.

In that role, I formed casual relationships with residents, which made them feel safe in opening up. As their time on earth neared a close, they unburdened their concerns. I learned to listen with my ears and heart, and to sense questions that would help dying people express their needs. This work honed my instincts for how to help them. It seemed I had a gift, so the staff started calling me in whenever they had residents nearing their transition.

I considered my most important work to be helping people find peace. It involves being oriented toward their needs and teaching their loved ones how to be supportive during a difficult time. I consider it to be a sacred space. I don't mean that in a religious sense, but it is a sensitive time, and it should focus on the transitioning person.

As much as I had learned from being around people in the final stages of their lives, I had never been tested at my core with personal grief. That was about to change.

Just before we moved, I went to see my maternal grandmother, Ursie. As I gathered my things to leave, I put my arms around her in a long embrace. While we hugged, strong impressions flooded me that this would be the last time to see her alive.

Then, the strangest thing happened. Time stood still. People use that expression, but I experienced it. It was as if all the particles slowed down and moved in slow motion. It felt like everything went still.

She was in good health, so my heart ached

at the foreboding sense that she might have a sudden health event, and I wouldn't make it back. However, my sadness mixed with gratitude that I was being gifted the knowledge that we were saying goodbye. It felt precious to memorize that hug. Many others do not get as much.

"Going to church" in Colorado

Richard

While recovering our losses in Woodland Park, Colorado, everything felt hard, like I was leaning into the wind just to stay upright. The Tanya Tucker song, "Two Sparrows in a Hurricane," felt like it was written for Laurrana and me.

We found solace in discovering a mountain meadow not far from where we lived, and it became one of our favorite places to get grounded. We called it "Going to church."

One afternoon, we ambled along the meadow's edge away from the marshy middle, and I felt the warmth of the sun on my skin. Fat bumblebees buzzed around the wildflowers as long grasses swayed. The scent of pinecones and herbs filled the crisp alpine air.

We spotted a granite boulder with a flat top,

so we sat together. Above, a red-tailed hawk circled on the hunt, backlit by the bluest sky and chunky clouds magnificently rolling in. These sights and sounds filled our minds, emptying us of whatever troubles had weighed on us earlier in the day.

I closed my eyes, and words came to my mind, as though in conversation.

The Voice: What are you doing?

This caught me totally by surprise.

Me: I'm not sure what you mean.

The Voice: What are you doing with yourself right now?

Me: I am working on myself to be a more spiritual person.

The Voice: How much of a spirit-being do you think you are, 80 percent? 85 percent?

There was a pause as I contemplated the question.

The Voice: Your spirit being is already one hundred percent spirit. It is impossible to be more than that.

Me: Okay, then what is spiritual growth? What can I do?

The Voice: You can increase your awareness of our relationship.

When we stood up to go, I had received the

guidance I needed. I returned home from the meadow knowing that I was already one with all that is.

Intense grief

Laurrana

A few months after moving to Colorado, Richard and I were walking in our meadow. It was our anniversary, and we were feeling content in each other's company.

Then, all at once, an overwhelming sense of foreboding came over me. My knees buckled, my body chilled, and I dropped to the ground, unable to continue on our walk for a time. Richard grabbed his coat and put it over my shoulders to comfort me. We immediately made our way back to the car and headed home. Once inside the house, I had a feeling to call my parents.

My dad answered, and when he heard my voice, he said, "Are you coming?"

Baffled, I said, "What do you mean, *coming?* What happened?"

He assumed I had called after hearing the news from someone else. Then he revealed the horrific news that my beloved grandmother, Ursie, had been murdered in cold blood. She was ninety-two and had been living in a nice, gated apartment building with onsite security. Some building maintenance people had done work on her place earlier in the day, and later, someone entered her apartment without force and stabbed her to death.

Although I had been waiting for the news of her passing since our last embrace, I felt more than sadness at this terrible news. This was *anguish*. I was broken open by the weight. Although I had known I would soon lose her, I was wholly unprepared for the shock and anger I felt. Her murder is a senseless tragedy that remains an unsolved cold case to this day. According to the local newspaper at the time, it was the most brutal murder in the history of her town.

Since then, I have worked through those first raw emotions, but it's still difficult to think about. The experience gave me even more empathy when people experience loss, and it taught me a lot about what *not* to say.

More than one person told me, "You should be grateful she lived a full life."

I wanted to snap back that I was grateful, but that doesn't remove my anger that her life ended by violence. It is possible to feel conflicting emotions at the same time. I ached for her fear and suffering in those last moments. My eyes stung with tears because she deserved a dignified death. We were robbed of hearing her last words. My anger signaled that the way she died wasn't right.

Others have said things like, "It has been two years. You should be over it by now."

Grief knows no timeline. I can appreciate when people who lose children say, "You never get over the pain, you just get used to the pain."

Even now, as I have spent time with countless families in preparing for death, I know that understanding the process does not soften the blow of grief when it happens to you.

Moving back to Las Vegas

Richard

After ten healing years in Colorado, new work opportunities opened up in Silicon Valley. Rapid development was in full swing, and with it, an overabundance of electrician work for me. We also felt guided there so we could be near Laurrana's family, especially because her mother was nearing the end of life. Her father was still living and took wonderful care of her, but The Voice had whispered that time was precious. So we went.

On our anniversary in 2001, Laurrana was

making dinner when I cranked up the radio's volume. It was the nightly Delilah program we sometimes listened to, and she dedicated a song from me to Laurrana for our anniversary. Then the station played Van Morrison's "Have I Told You Lately That I Love You." Her eyes filled with tears. She could never hear that song without getting emotional.

By mid-2002, both of our children had enlisted in the military, making us very proud of their choices and excited to see how they would grow. The military had not been the right path for me, but we wholeheartedly supported their choice.

In late 2002, my father called one day saying, "Son, I'm going to be in San Francisco for a convention. I'd like you and Laurrana to come stay at the Hotel Fairmont and attend the family day."

He was the featured speaker, and it felt like a great privilege to be there with him and see people lined up around the block. They wanted to thank him for all the service he had given to the profession. I think it meant a lot that his son could see that. Parents crave the feeling that their kids are proud of them, just like children need to feel that their parents are proud. I did feel that way about him.

While attending that event, someone I knew approached me about a job opening as Compliance

Director of Southern Nevada IBEW/NECA-LMCC in Las Vegas. It felt serendipitous, and the dominoes fell quickly after that. By then, I was happy to move back to be near my dad. Moving back to my hometown, my life was coming full circle.

Later, I was promoted to serve as the Executive Director, the position I held when I retired.

The flow

Laurrana

One thing Richard and I have learned is not to fight when energy isn't flowing. There are so many books in our culture telling people to fight no matter what. Everything seems to be about, "You can do it!"

But it's foolish to try pushing a river. Yes, when you feel called to do something, it's important not to give up. But there's a difference between grit and fighting against what you feel energetically. Our culture and work ethic came out of the machine age, and that's about dominating, not following the divine plan. Once you sense a deeper divine plan, it's time to stop trying to force the outcome you want.

At other times, the energy does flow. Our move back to Las Vegas was that way. We bought a home, and Richard entered a rewarding phase of his career. After our son finished his enlistment with the military, he serendipitously got a wonderful job. He and his family moved just minutes away. Being back in Las Vegas also helped Richard and his dad build new connections they'd never enjoyed together before.

However, when we first got there, I was struggling because I didn't know anyone, and my career had been uprooted. My mother passed away not long before we left the Bay Area, and I was grieving her loss deeply.

One day, I saw a job announcement for a "Comfort Care Coordinator" without an explanation of what it entailed. I felt a nudge to apply. When I got an interview, I learned I would be working for a large hospice organization that wanted to help people with their transition in innovative new ways. Very few organizations nationally were doing anything like what they envisioned, so I explained my perspective and the modalities I had picked up through my career. The woman interviewing me had tears in her eyes. "You are exactly what we want. I believe you were sent to us."

In retrospect, I can see that shortly after my mother passed away, new opportunities began opening up for me. I had been struggling with the loss, and I believe she saw what I needed and helped me find that job. It came together so effortlessly. It turned out to be exactly what I needed in so many ways, and it was a true calling. In helping people work through their emotions, my heart healed.

I created a program to help patients transitioning at the end of life, their families, and the medical staff who supported them. That program was very successful and is still in use today. In the coming years, other hospice organizations would hire me to do similar work. I knew my efforts were helping people when word got out and I started getting calls from physicians who had patients that needed help.

These people had "spiritual restlessness," which is a term I coined for when a patient is experiencing discomfort or anxiousness even after having every physical need met.

Later in my career, I gave trainings to help other nurses know how they can serve people who are dying. I taught that we should observe if they are restless. Then, we allow that person to share what their needs are. Sometimes they will share a regret.

For example, I remember one man who seemed like he would have passed sooner. I sat at his bedside and asked, "How are you feeling about things right now?"

He said, "I have one regret. I've been estranged from my siblings for twenty years and haven't seen them. They're my only living relatives, and I wish I had a way to talk to them before I leave."

I said, "Really? Where do they live?"

He told me, and I asked their names. We then arranged for them to fly in. He was able to say his final goodbyes after all that time. He died right after that, and they wrote me and the other staff touching notes to say thank you.

I could tell hundreds of touching stories like that, about ways our hospice work helped people resolve regrets or have spiritual breakthroughs before their passing. It was deeply meaningful work.

One Breath

Chapter Four: The Event

Life before the event
Richard

September 24, 2022 was the best kind of day, celebratory in an ordinary sort of way. The Las Vegas heat had cooled into fall as Laurrana and I went to the annual electrician's picnic at Floyd Lamb Park. I had first attended that same annual picnic with my dad when I was eight years old. We felt at home in this group of colleagues and friends. I had recently retired after fourteen years in the job that fell into my lap while attending the retirement convention with my dad. I'd spent fifty years in my career as an electrician since Hawaii.

Laurrana and I mingled, watched children at play, and enjoyed some good old-fashioned barbecue. We were having a great time, but I had to sit down and catch my breath occasionally. For several years, I'd noticed a loss of stamina and had not felt like doing much. This was a big change from how active we had always been, prioritizing our health. We ate well, exercised, rarely had even a social drink, and never smoked cigarettes. Other than some brief experimentation with marijuana and psychedelics in the 60s, our lifestyle had been very clean. We always took high-quality vitamin and mineral supplements. Daily meditation has taken us to much higher planes than any substances ever did or could.

Earlier in September, we had gone for a wilderness hike at Red Rock Canyon National Conservation Area, and the weather had been spectacular. We always enjoy hiking and talking to people on the trails, but I had been unusually wiped out.

I saw my doctor, and he determined that my cholesterol was good, even on the low end of the spectrum, and my white blood cell count was low, too.

He thought I looked pretty good for my age and was not concerned. So, I chalked up the changes to being in my early seventies. Now that I was in another age bracket, some decline was to be expected.

The evening after the picnic, our ten-year-old granddaughter came over to spend the night while our son, Shean, and his wife went to a Las Vegas concert. We played a game of Scrabble, munched on pizza and frozen yogurt while she caught us up on all the Taylor Swift news. It was a treat having her live nearby since our other grandchildren were abroad.

To stay close to our daughter and grandchildren, we had a weekly tradition of video chats. We looked forward to getting caught up on what our granddaughters were doing in school and with their activities. They'd often tell us of outings, especially exploring all that nature offers. Our preschool-aged grandson always wanted to show me his toy cars and trucks, and for me to see how cool they are. His vocabulary was really growing.

During that time, we were feeling so proud of how both of our children were raising their children. We tried to bring up our son and daughter the way we wished our parents had been with us. That's not a criticism of our parents—they came from a different era, and we recognize how fortunate we both were to come from such good families. But Laurrana and I had another vision for our family. Now that our children were parents, we could see they were doing an even better job than we had done with them. I can't think of anything more rewarding than that.

In early October, Shean surprised me with an early combined birthday present. We shared a birthday month, so he took me to a Las Vegas Raiders v. Denver Broncos football game at the new Allegiant Stadium. It was my first time there, and we had a great time. I loved making new father-son memories.

By this time, however, I felt truly unwell. Since we had already been to several specialists, I was referred to a cancer center for an injection to stimulate white blood cell production. In the coming days, I noticed unusual sensations in my body, and so I went back for a follow-up visit on October 7. I felt so dizzy that day that Laurrana had to drive. Still, they couldn't find anything, so they made a referral for us to see a liver specialist to explore other causes. We went home with no more answers.

The Event

Richard

On the evening of October 10, Laurrana and I

were in the living room watching television when I felt my body flooded with a strange sensation.

"Honey, I think I need to go lie down." I stood and felt woozy.

She glanced up on high alert. She could tell something was wrong.

"Would you help steady me?"

She stood so I could place my hands on her shoulders. We took one step, and then I collapsed to the floor, taking her down with me.

Her phone slid out of her hand as we toppled. She freed herself from underneath me and called Shean. He arrived just minutes later and helped get me into bed.

Shean said, "I think you should go to emergency."

"Nah," I replied. "I've got my doctor appointment first thing."

He seemed exasperated but resigned to my wishes. They got me into bed, and he went home.

Laurrana crawled in next to me, almost begging me to go to the hospital, but I thought the E.R. would be just as unlikely to find anything as the other doctors had been. We should wait it out until morning when the specialists could take a look.

"I just need to rest. It's only a few more hours."

"We're not doing that."

Laurrana

I watched Richard closely all evening because I recognized the signs of how dire the situation was. Color drained from his face, and his breathing was labored. I urged him to let me take him to the E.R., but he was adamant. Did he truly believe he would be fine until morning?

I worried that instead of thinking he would be fine, he might already sense his time on earth closing and did not want to tell me. Maybe it was even on a subconscious level, and he didn't want to leave our peaceful home for a chaotic hospital environment. Maybe he wanted to die at home.

Paying attention to what Richard wanted overrode what I wanted. Hospice work taught me to notice and honor the wishes of each individual. I don't believe in interfering. My role is to help someone have what we call in the business, "a good death." This is one of my most sacred values.

I could have cajoled him into going, but instead was thinking, If Richard's life ends tonight, we will not spend our last moments arguing. We're not doing that.

Instead, I felt a peace that I was competent enough to help him cross over without interference from me. I would not whip up a frenzy of anxious energy. Instead, I set about creating the most beautiful, comforting space possible. My entire career had prepared me for that moment.

But sometime around 2 a.m., he slipped out of consciousness for a few minutes. When he woke up, I finally felt the spirit prompt me to call 9-1-1 and said so to Richard. He nodded in consent.

I had just enough time to grab his medical information before they were at our door. I couldn't believe how fast the ambulance arrived, almost like it had been parked and ready outside our house. No sirens or lights, they just appeared in a blink.

When they rushed inside, I whispered to the paramedics, "He's actively dying."

They nodded, "Yeah." They could see it, too.

I handed them his medical records, and they asked, "Are you a doctor or something? Nobody ever gives us this."

Another one told me not to come for a half hour because "They have to check him in."

I have never changed my clothes so fast in my life. Then I sprinted to my car and rode the ambulance's bumper to the hospital, only a few blocks away. The doors flew open, and a team raced Richard into the emergency room, instructing me to follow them in.

I called Shean and said, "Honey, I'm sorry. I know you just got home, but I had to bring your dad to the hospital."

He said, "I never should have let him talk me out of that. I'll be right there."

I assured him, "No, it's okay. It's going to be okay."

I believed those words, even if "okay" meant it was Richard's time to go.

The death experience

Richard

The last thing I remembered that night was a team of paramedics with a gurney alongside my bed. They were pulling me onto a slide board and then onto the gurney. I heard a paramedic say, "One, two, three," then I felt my head snap to one side at the movement. Then I lost consciousness. I was no longer "here."

As my body lay motionless on the emergency-room bed, I found myself—that is, the timeless, ageless, spirit part of myself—floating in the middle of an infinite ocean of energy. My eyes were open, but I could not see my nose because I was not in my physical body.

58

I marveled at all the glowing, plasma-like energy surrounding me. I viewed it in sharp focus in every direction. There was no end to it, no beginning, no top, and no bottom. I pondered how interesting it was from a dimensional perspective because it seemed beyond the laws of spatial physics; it was more than 3-D.

Then, I became concerned that I was not breathing.

How could I be in an ocean without breathing?

I didn't know where I was, but I knew my physical body was somewhere else, and it needed to breathe. Yet, it did not worry me because I felt a vast and overpowering peace that quelled any worries. My concern for my body was dissipating.

Instead, I became wrapped in complete, unconditional acceptance. That acceptance felt comfortable and yet magnificent, all-powerful, and divine. I sensed I was in the epicenter of all love. This was the Source of all that is. I was in the palm of God's hand.

And then it felt like this "God Ocean" was waiting, waiting for me to make a move. Would I stay there and forever merge with the Source? My energy was shifting.

I thought, *I can be this,* meaning that I could

just remain there and become one with it.

Then, as soon as I thought of remaining there, poof, I wasn't there. It was like the thought had caused my spirit to move in an ever-so-slight intention away from the nucleus of the "God Ocean." And with that flicker of movement, I was traveling.

And yet, I still felt the center of the God Ocean within me. I had moved, but the center did not part ways. The ocean was infinite and vast, but also within me.

I traveled to a place that felt betwixt and between. I wondered, *Where am I?* It was a curious question because I was no longer in the middle of the God Ocean, and I was not inside my physical body either.

The space around me began coming into focus. I was now in an earthly room. I couldn't clearly make out what was going on in the peripheral room, which seemed fuzzy and small compared to the wide-open space of the cosmos. All my attention focused on someone standing about ten feet away, a woman. She was tall and had dark, long hair. She wore a softly hooded white robe with blue trim, looking straight at me, straight into me.

Her voice called out my name in a fierce but loving tone, "Richard!"

Then she repeated it, trying to get my attention, "Richard!"

Why was she calling my name? I was confused. What did she want?

"Richard!"

I felt myself slipping into a state of blissful calm. I was succumbing to the peaceful hush of the God Ocean.

"Richard!"

She brought my attention back. Now I became intent on figuring out what was going on. I tried harder to focus my attention on her again. When I did, a moment of recognition dawned on me.

I know you. Mother Mary.

Then, in response to my recognition, she rose up, as if on her toes. She lasered her attention straight at me. There was an urgency in her voice, no time for greetings or for me to be awestruck by her presence.

This time she screamed my name, "RICHARD!"

At her command, my heart jolted awake. I took a breath. With that gasp, my spirit came back into my body, and I was "here" again. Mary was gone.

She had sent me back by sheer command of her voice. I wasn't asked what I wanted; Mary had ordered me.

My body started breathing again, but I would lie unconscious in a coma for several more days. The Universe had more to show me.

I am a widow

Laurrana

When the hospital E.R. staff invited me into the room, I felt God's hand in the situation, because they do not usually do that.

I stood at the foot of Richard's bed, helplessly watching these expert E.R. veterans working in their element. I had spent plenty of time in hospital rooms, but not in an intense situation like this. That is because there are no extreme measures to save someone's life when someone is on hospice. Death comes quietly.

This was not loud, but very intense. The doctor narrated terrifying updates like "severe shock" and "cardiac arrest." I saw the patient electronic monitor go flat.

Then, it started up again.

And then it went flat again, staying that way. No heartbeat.

The team performed chest compressions, not giving up. But I was prepared to accept the inevitable.

Richard was gone.

I am a widow, I thought. I was stunned. At that moment, my heart broke in two. It was as if every bit of sorrow and heartbreak I had ever experienced was pouring out of me. It was the most excruciating emotional pain I have ever felt in my life, and the enormity of it made me question whether I might emotionally survive it. I simultaneously felt tremendous sorrow and tremendous love for him. I wanted to slump to my knees because the weight of what had happened was pushing me downward. It felt like too much to bear standing.

Yet, somehow, I was not afraid. It's strange how your mind can process multiple threads of information at once. I tried to absorb the blow of losing my husband, yet my career in hospice had also trained me with the muscle memory to be present for these moments, and I was. Despite my sorrow, I stood ready for however I might be needed.

Then, something peculiar happened, similar to when I was told it would be the last time to see my grandmother alive. Time slowed in the room, and a calming peace swept over me. I watched the hospital staff move as if in slow motion. It reminded me of the people I have seen at the park doing tai chi, flowing in harmonious synchronicity.

All at once, I saw a radiant burst of light shoot out from my heart and across the room. I can't explain it, but it was visible to my eyes, like a spotlight beaming onto where Richard lay.

The instant it hit him, his mouth opened, and he took in a gasping breath.

I felt a surge of joy and relief. *We were receiving more time.*

But then, almost simultaneously, my mind leaped forward to the next phase. What is the situation now? Will his brain be damaged? Will he still be the same Richard?

They put him on life support, and I still didn't know what we were dealing with. I sat in vigil beside him through the rest of that day and all night as he lay intubated on a ventilator in the intensive care unit, or ICU. He was unconscious but had a pleasant expression on his face. I was really struggling, though, and I passed some of the time by journaling little love notes to Richard in my phone. No amount of training in the field of death and dying will make it so you don't feel all the hard feelings when times like this strike you.

The next day, the attending physician came in to explain to me and Shean what had happened.

I wanted straight, clinical answers, but Shean was more sensitive in that moment.

Shean implored me, "Mom, *stop*. Dad can hear us. Let's not scare him or leap too far ahead."

He later also expressed that he did not want our time to be spoiled by what *might be* rather than being present to what his dad needed.

Shean was right, and we then moved our conversation to a more private space.

The doctor was candid. "Most people don't survive what your husband went through."

I nodded. "I could tell he was actively dying. I've spent my career in hospice."

"Ah. Then you know how serious this was. I will explain what happened the way I would to any patient's family, although you probably already know a lot of this."

He continued. "Richard had a blood vessel burst in his esophagus. We call it a GI bleed, and it is an extremely urgent and dangerous condition because it causes severe internal bleeding. A lot of patients don't even make it to the hospital. It's difficult to stop it fast enough."

I asked, "Do you know what caused it?"

The doctor referred to a folder on the counter and shook his head. "It happened when a blood vessel called a varix burst. Varices are swollen veins that form when the liver is scarred and can't handle blood flow properly. Think of them as weak, balloon-like spots in the veins that can pop under pressure. When one burst in Richard's esophagus, blood poured out rapidly. It's a critical situation because the ruptured varix is close to the heart, so every beat was pumping more blood directly into his stomach."

I felt baffled. "This is related to scarring in the liver? How could that be? Richard doesn't have the risk factors."

The doctor was warm, but I detected a hint of skepticism. "Scarring of the liver can occur from heavy drinking, hepatitis, or fatty liver from diet. I don't see any of that on his chart. What do you know?"

I was emphatic. "Richard has such a clean lifestyle. He's never been a drinker, and we have a healthy diet. No hepatitis."

The doctor noted in his clipboard, "Patient reports no history of alcohol."

I glanced at his notes, understanding that he was leaving room for doubt because people often underreport alcohol use. I stood by my statement. Richard and I knew everything about each other. We later learned that diabetes is a risk factor that Richard has. In retrospect, it seemed like a big marker, but the body is complex, and it is easy for doctors to miss things.

The doctor continued, "He's not out of the woods yet. We will monitor him closely because if there was one bubble, there could be more. As soon as he is stable, we will perform a technique called banding. This is where we close off weak veins with rubber bands. It blocks them and creates scar tissue to prevent further bleeds."

That night, Shean and I left to sleep in our own beds. We both needed rest, and hospitals are not restful places. When I entered our home, however, an overwhelming wave of emptiness washed over me. Everywhere I looked, I saw Richard. The thought occurred to me *that we'd been together since we were practically kids. We grew up together. I don't know how to be on my own.*

My heart ached, and I felt abandoned by the universe. I felt like I was twenty-one again in the time before we met.

Who am I without him? I was a child.

I shuffled through the house, and my eyes landed on a fancy new thermostat Richard had just installed. *I have no idea how to use it*, I thought. My stomach knotted at the idea of just how many tasks Richard had always taken care of, big and little chores I didn't know how to do.

I stood at the threshold of our bedroom and

hesitated before stepping inside. I looked at his cold side of the bed, then buried my head in the pillow and wept. It was the deepest grief I have ever felt.

I couldn't imagine getting any sleep there. After about fifteen minutes, I found the silence unbearable and called Shean.

"I'm so sorry, but..." I choked on a sob. It took me a minute to regain my composure. "I can't stay here. I want to be where your dad is. I'm driving back."

He said, "No, you're not. I'm coming to drive you."

I said, "That's ridiculous. The hospital is around the corner. It's six minutes."

He won the argument. On the way, I was apologetic, but he reassured me it was no trouble. He expressed what a privilege it was to be there whenever and however I needed him.

I don't know what I would have done without him and our daughter during that time. His boss had said to him, "Don't worry about work right now. Don't even think about this place. Just do what you have to do."

Our daughter called me at least once every night to get updates and offer questions to ask Richard's doctors. She gave me immense support amidst her own uncertainty. I know that when you're not there in person, your mind can jump to the worst because you think other people may be shielding you from the truth. So, she had to imagine what was going on, and she must have been in knots about it. Yet, she stepped up and allowed me to lean on her during that tender time. I was touched to see the character of both our daughter and son shine.

On the third day, they transferred Richard into a private room where four IV poles dripped life into him. Monitors beeped everywhere. It was time to take him off life support. They said they did not know what kind of damage his organs or brain had sustained. We would not know what the situation was until they removed the ventilator. Then we would see if he could breathe on his own. If he took in the breath of life without mechanical support, then he had a fighting chance.

Before they unplugged the ventilator, they ran a slate of tests. When they went over the results, the tone I felt was, "We have done all we can do for now. We just have to see what happens."

They did not tell us this, but his medical records later revealed a GCS coma score of 3, which indicates the most severe level of unconsciousness. He was totally unresponsive. Before the event, his liver was already in advanced stages of shutting down, a condition that had been worsening for years without us realizing it. If he survived off life support, he could have brain damage and might need a liver transplant.

They removed the ventilator with Shean present. When Richard first came to, he was weaning off a lot of medications, delirious, and frantic. His suffering gutted me, but at least he was alive. The doctors told us he could relapse at any time.

I sent out a text to our loved ones that read:

> *Today was a good day. Richard was taken off heavy sedation. They wanted to see how he would tolerate it. In addition, before removing the breathing tube could take place, he needed to be awake enough to follow commands, and he did. Fortunately, once the breathing tube was removed, he was able to breathe on his own. He even began talking a blue streak! So in all, it was a very positive sign. He was fully aware we were there. Richard had the nurses laughing with all the jokes and stories he was telling*

*them. Thanks for your prayers
and support. Please keep them
coming. He is grateful for your
well-wishes.*

I remained positive, but still couldn't help but worry that nothing would ever be the same. I grieved the loss of our future, and so I prayed continually. "Please help me. I need divine presence. Please come show me what I need to know and do." I called upon so much help from the other side.

A lot happened in those first days.

In love with love

Richard

The first moments of waking up were anxious and disorienting as I transitioned back into my body. After that transition and fully coming to my senses, I found myself in a hospital room, immersed in a state of bliss. I was still bathed in love that came from the ocean of energy. I felt only love. I breathed love. I fell in love with love, which was everywhere—the most universal force there is. That's all there was for me during that time, subtle yet strong. Powerful yet gentle. It was infinite beyond words.

During that time, I had no awareness of all that Laurrana was doing for me. Spiritually, she was holding a private, prayerful vigil that I might fully return to the living with a heart that would remain open to receive whatever there was to learn from the experience. Physically, she was making sure that all my medical needs were attended to, putting my needs above her own rest.

They attached me to four IV poles that the staff called Christmas trees, and during that time, I would receive nineteen transfusions. A bank of support monitors continuously tracked my vitals.

My mind drifted in and out of wakefulness. I felt awe in the sensation of my breath, like it was the first time I had ever noticed it. With every breath, I felt the Divine Mother's spirit. I sensed an energy swirling around the ceiling of my room, and I could feel Mother Mary's presence there, working intensely on my body, mind, and soul. She was keeping me alive.

One night, an elderly woman was admitted to my floor. I did not see her, but I could hear her loudly wailing and telling her daughter, who flew in from out of state, that she was dying of cancer and her time on earth was short. I'm sure that the whole hospital could hear her. She begged her daughter to stay with her in her room to the end; however, the daughter told her mom that she had to leave, and the daughter left the room to fly home. The woman wailed out of deep-seated fear and loneliness. I called upon "The Voice" to comfort this woman with divine love. Then I recited the Lord's Prayer and added my own words, asking for her to be comforted. Just as the last syllable was on the tip of my tongue, her wailing instantly stopped. I was shocked. Almost three years have gone by, and this event has stayed with me as if it happened last night.

Throughout this time, I felt inextricably connected to spirit and was engaged in ongoing conversations with The Voice. I used to call it God, but now I have started calling it "The Divine Consciousness."

Here is one of the more vivid conversations.

The Voice: What do you think about what just happened to you?

Me: I sure was fortunate that the new hospital was built so close to my house.

The Voice: Oh.

Me: Also, what a lucky coincidence that they just built a new fire station halfway between the house and the new hospital. The first responders got to me fast. And it was so fortunate I flatlined in the hospital and not somewhere else because every extra minute can cause complications.

The Voice: Oh, coincidence.

Me: So, not coincidence?

The Voice then walked me through a short conversation to help me grasp with a conscious understanding that everything in my life had been orchestrated—all the perceived coincidences, the hospital so near our home, the close fire department, the fast ambulance response, the expert skills of the emergency-room attendants, the smooth work of hands—everything. It was a divine plan, and the only plan in action.

The Voice further explained that all the events in my life from childhood through adulthood had led up to my death experience. The Voice instructed me that I must not judge any moments from my life as right or wrong. There had never been judgment upon me—*none whatsoever*. Rather, all experiences had presented me with the gift of opportunity. Experiences were a chance for me to grow a conscious connection with the divine Source. Everything that happened was a chance to grow, develop, and increase my awareness of *all that is*. Everything that had happened in my life was building to this experience and preparing me to receive it. There had been no accidents or mistakes.

The Voice made it abundantly clear that there is no separation between me and the Source of all that is. *None.* I must let go of any notion of separation that I might be clinging to.

The Voice asked, How do you feel about Mother Mary's presence?

Me: I feel humbly and deeply blessed by her powerful omnipresence. She is so very present right now.

The Voice: What have you learned about Jesus?

Me: In my childhood, Jesus taught me when to pray, how to pray, and where to bow. Jesus taught me to follow his lead and to pray to the same God that he prayed to.

The Voice: I am what flows through Jesus and Mary. Jesus and Mary are pure channels of love.

I drifted into sleep.

When I awoke, I understood that Jesus and Mary were symbols of Divine Consciousness. It now made sense that when people have near-death experiences, they might be visited by a different being of light. Was one experience more true than the other? No, people receive the messages they are most prepared to receive.

A nurse entered my room and seemed to linger beyond what was necessary. I got the feeling she wanted to hang out with me for a while. I think there was an energy she could feel.

I glanced toward the empty chair where Laurrana usually sat. The nurse noticed and said, "She went home to shower."

I noticed after that how other staff seemed to linger with me, too. I would show them the picture of Mary that Laurrana had put up, and I'd tell them how Mary was the reason I survived. (In reality, it had been two guardian women who saved me, Mary and Laurrana, but I did not yet know about the beam of light that connected the two of us the moment I returned.)

I told my story with such childlike exuberance that it was contagious.

When Laurrana returned, I introduced her to the nurse, who looked puzzled. "Then who was that other woman?"

I said, "That was also my wife."

We had a good laugh. Laurrana had been so exhausted and harried that when she came back all showered and freshened up, she looked like a different person. To me, my wife was always a beautiful woman, whether or not she had makeup on.

When the nurse left, Laurrana said, "I've been thinking about how October 10 was the day of your death. It was also the birthday of Richard Version 2."

After all the talking, I drifted into sleep and had another conversation. In this one, The Voice asked a fresh series of questions.

The Voice: How do you feel about everything now?

Me: All I feel is love, all I know is love. I'm in love with love!

The Voice: What about everything else?

Me: My head and heart are just swimming in love, and I don't want anything to take me out of my heart. I don't care about anything else.

The Voice: Do you know why you aren't concerned? Because my hand is in everything. ***Everything.***

Me: I understand. I'm not intoxicated with love; it's that now I see how God is in everything. There is no separation. Now I can feel love everywhere.

Then it hit me: God is The Voice. God is love. Love is everywhere.

The Voice: And???

Me: Oh! You want me to flip it. OK. God is love, and love is everywhere. Therefore, love is God, and God is everywhere. God is synonymous with love. And Love is synonymous with God.

Through that conversation, I understood that anything that touches our heart with goodness is

God. It could be a butterfly, a song, or a pet. It could be sunshine, a flower, or an act of kindness. When we give love, and when we receive love, it's all God. Love is the most powerful force, and we are touched by it all the time.

I was beginning to realize that I needed time in the hospital not only for my body to recover, but to remain in a sacred space of transition between worlds until I understood all that I needed. It was a time of bringing the truths I felt from the God Ocean into my conscious mind so I could find words for them. The Voice wouldn't let up until I got it. It was a process of bringing nebulous feelings into my conscious awareness.

The Voice: You need to get all this.

I wasn't going home until I did.

In another conversation, The Voice led me down an important path of understanding.

The Voice: Do you remember a conversation we had a year ago?

Me: It had to do with my beliefs around what will happen when I exhale my last breath, and what happened when I inhaled my first breath of life, and every breath in between.

The Voice: OK, so now understand this. I am the inhale. I am the breath. You are the inhale. You are the breath. There is no separation! There is an infinite/finite inhale/exhale. There is no separation.

Me: I am the Inhale, I am the breath - I am the exhale, I am the breath. This will be my mantra.

In my waking times, I pondered the meaning of breath further. Life begins with the first breath and ends with the last. In between, when we react to stress, we might get tense, and our breath shortens. We tell each other to "just breathe," or "take a deep breath, and you will feel that everything will be alright."

There is more going on than we realize! If we understand our creator inhales and exhales each breath with us, there truly is no separation. We are never alone.

Our conscious mind doesn't even know that it's happening, but we can use our free will to become aware of the breath. We can embrace the calm feeling of bliss, as subtle as a kiss from a butterfly.

Later, The Voice sprinkled another layer of wisdom on top of my new mantra.

The Voice: Release the burden of yesterday and tomorrow. Today is all there is. There was no right or wrong in your past, only a path that led you to today.

Before October 10, 2022, I had thoughts and beliefs. I'd spent a lifetime developing my spirituality. After my experience, my beliefs were replaced with reality. The unknown became known to me.

The next ten days

Laurrana

Richard had eaten nothing since dinnertime at home before *the event*, and now five days had passed. He was getting nutrition from a drip, but he felt really hungry by then and was losing weight fast. So, I went on a mission to fix that immediate problem. They kept telling me that there was one doctor who needed to clear Richard for solid food, but he was not returning the staff's phone calls.

Meanwhile, Richard was what they call "A hard stick," meaning that the phlebotomists had great difficulty drawing blood. Although he remained calm spiritually, I could see the stress his body was under. His face winced every time he could hear one of them coming, and he commented privately to me that he could practically feel his veins cringing away from them, like worms from a fishing hook. He knew they were unlikely to hit a vein the first time; they'd have to poke and poke and poke.

We warned them he was a tough case in hopes they would only have the most experienced people try. Sometimes, they left to get nurses from the onsite laboratory services or surgical services because they were superb at it. One of them noticed how paper-thin his skin had become and that the bandages were removing skin. She told us about Coban tape, which was a godsend. It sticks to itself but does not damage delicate skin. From then on, we had a roll in the drawer and instructed the nurses to use it exclusively.

Still, he brightened when nurses and even the phlebotomists came into the room. He cracked jokes and tried to get a smile out of them. When they asked, "Do you smoke?" He'd say, "Only if you light me on fire." Some didn't know what to make of his sense of humor, but they all seemed to enjoy visiting with him.

I could see how he willed himself to treat them kindly and not take out his frustrations. They were just doing a job.

Finally, on the sixth day, I tracked down the doctor in charge of Richard's dietary restrictions. He answered, "Oh yeah, how long has it been? He's fine to eat now."

A few minutes later, an orderly presented Richard with a Thanksgiving-style feast. He had the widest grin and attacked it with gusto, although he could only eat a small portion of what they had brought. You'd have thought they were feeding a sumo wrestler.

On the seventh day, they wanted to move

Richard out of the hospital and into a rehab facility. A hospital floor manager thought Richard was well enough to move and insisted that he either return home or to an inpatient rehabilitation center, but I told them I didn't think he was well enough to go. Later, I would kick myself because I had the training to know I could have refused discharge. But I was exhausted and didn't have the presence of mind to put my foot down.

The next ambulance ride

Richard

A hospital administrator arranged for me to go to a local inpatient rehabilitation center that they frequently used. That afternoon, I was transported to the inpatient rehabilitation center by ambulance. I got checked in and was shown to a room.

Most of the people working there were students or independent contractors and were not as professional as the hospital staff had been. Nevertheless, they had equipment that my home did not have, so I was glad to at least have access to that.

After arriving, the R.N. ordered a portable full chest scan to see what was going on. I slept there overnight, and first thing in the morning, an independent traveling technician showed up with his

82

portable scan device.

He was the only person in the room. He manipulated my bed to lay me out as flat as possible and spread some gel on my chest. Then, he laid a large, flat, and rather heavy plate on my chest. The moment he did, I could feel my throat filling up rapidly with warm fluid. I was bleeding out again. I knew I had only a few seconds before I could not speak, then breathe, and then I would lose consciousness.

I couldn't shout, so I frantically waved my arms and grunted. He looked at me like I was a crazy man. He was panicking, and froze instead of springing into action. I mustered everything I had to yell NURSE! He responded by calling out, "NURSE!" My room quickly filled with students and untrained people who were freaking out all around me.

One student ran out and brought back a nurse, who immediately propped me upright. Then she stepped out into the hall and yelled for the nurse in charge, who had the authority to make decisions. The "charge nurse" on duty came running in and yelled at everybody to calm down. She barked out commands and told the others to keep me sitting up at all costs, and to get me into an ambulance, *stat*.

"Coincidentally," there was an ambulance right outside my room in the parking lot. I could see it from my window. It had just dropped someone else off at this facility, and it was sitting there taking a break before going back on the road.

The staff swiftly wheeled me out to the waiting ambulance, and the E.M.T.s adjusted the rig to keep me sitting upright. The nurse told them I was a GI bleed and to get me to Dignity San Martin, just 3.6 miles away. They sped with lights and sirens blazing. This time, I was awake for everything, hearing the E.M.T. working on me call out my vitals to another one who relayed the information to the hospital emergency room.

I heard one say, "That makes our second GI Bleed of the day." I do not know whether the other one made it, but in that moment, I did not know if I would.

It's quite something to be in a situation where your life is hanging in the balance and you are totally cognizant of it. My first bleed-out had led to unconsciousness and my death, but I was wide awake for this close call.

Yet, I was still in too much of a state of bliss to be afraid. The thought of going back to the God Ocean was not without appeal. Now and then, I caught glimpses of Laurrana pacing past the window outside my room, and my heart ached. I was in no hurry to leave her and our children. I *wanted* to stay alive.

Nobody wins the lottery twice

Laurrana

Richard had been in the rehab facility for less than twenty-four hours when I went out to run some errands. I mapped my route from farthest to closest, ending up at the hospital where I needed to pick up his medical records. But as I left the house, I had the impression I should go to the hospital first, and so I changed my plans.

As I stood at the reception desk, my phone rang. The voice on the other end of the phone told me he was being rushed back to the hospital E.R. He'd just had a second bleed-out, and I should come to the hospital right away.

"I'm already here," I told them. "I had a feeling I needed to come here first."

I believe the spirit led me to be there already when he arrived. I rushed to the E.R., where an intake person came to ask me questions about his history. I said he had been discharged the day before. She replied, "We have no record of him being a patient."

"How can that be? He was here for over a week."

It took a lot of wrangling to figure out that

Richard's records were moved after his discharge and were now caught in limbo between departments. That meant the immediate responding team was flying blind. I tried explaining his history, but worried that details might get lost in translation. I also worried that my persistence in solving the problem would be perceived as a nuisance. I was managing extreme anxiety, wondering if my husband would live through this, trying to get his records located, and trying to treat everyone with empathy. It was too much, and my emotions were about to bubble over.

What happened next marked one of the worst traumas of the whole experience. They wouldn't let me anywhere near Richard. I knew what that meant. It meant they were trying to keep him alive because if he were alive and fine, they would bring me right in.

That told me he was dying again. In my mind, I was thinking, *Nobody hits the lottery twice.*

I called our son so he could be present in case his dad didn't make it.

I slumped into the waiting area, and the dam broke. Tears gushed out, and my body shook with sobs. Since Richard's first emergency, I'd had too much time to contemplate the empty house and the crushing aloneness I would feel without my soul mate and life partner. Richard and I had always talked about everything, and during these days, there was no way to share with him everything I was going through. While he had remained in a state of bliss, I couldn't help but balance my happiness for every moment with him, and anticipatory grief for what may be ahead. The extreme emotional swings I experienced during that entire period were overwhelmingly intense.

After gaining my composure enough to speak, I phoned one of my girlfriends and decompressed with her. All the while, my heart was in a constant state of prayer for divine help so I could be fully present. I needed to be my best self for my husband, my daughter, and my son.

The waiting felt endless as they worked on him. I didn't know what was happening.

I believe it was not a coincidence that an ambulance had been parked right outside the rehab facility. Every second was critical in saving his life. It also felt like divine providence that I was already at the hospital and not clear across town. Even though they did not let me into the room during his second bleed, it still meant the world to me that I was there. Yes, I would have been praying from afar once I got the call, but I also believe my physical presence in the hospital mattered. What if the love radiating from my heart contributed to the outcome, even in the slightest way?

What I know is that the margin between his living and dying had been razor thin.

Another immense blessing was when we learned that a new physician, Dr. Jeff Olsen, was taking the lead on his case. From the moment we met him, we knew we were in the best of hands. He was an all-star quarterback, and everything about Richard's care cleared through him from that moment on. No more premature dismissals, no more waiting for food orders. He would ensure the banding was done right, fixing the problem before Richard went home.

Meanwhile, we felt grateful for such a beautiful physical environment. Some hospitals seem like industrial complexes, chemically sanitized and fluorescently lit. San Martin Hospital was bathed in natural light and felt clean, like how a desert landscape is cleansed by the sun. Every detail encouraged healing and love. We observed the staff members as they worked, aligned in purpose. Designers had thoughtfully laid out the hospital to place each wing for optimal healing, privacy, and access for loved ones. Here are some examples.

Each morning, we heard a tone in the intercom calling the staff to start their day in prayer. Richard and I stopped whatever we were doing to pray with them and for them. At other random times during the day, a soft lullaby would play on the intercom. We asked a nurse what it was. She said, "That means a baby was just born. We like celebrating when a new life comes into the world."

We also knew that every day, some patients were struggling for their breath in the intensive care unit (ICU), and others were leaving this world. Richard's experience had attuned us to feel the energy present as other souls were taking their first and last breaths in close physical proximity. Even in my exhaustion and uncertainty, I felt the sacredness of those moments happening around us. It's hard to put into words just how tender and spiritually moving that whole time was.

Steps are not the destination

Richard

My hospital stay would soon be done. I lost a lot of muscle and gained a lot of swelling; my belly button was gone. I did not recognize my arms, which were so swollen I was afraid that if someone came in to stick me with a needle, I would pop.

Shean visited one day and sat close to me, holding my hand between his.

He said, "Dad, I just want you to know that

you have been the dad to me that you always wanted to have."

I was blown away by his maturity and depth of thought.

Then he added, "And I am the son you always wanted to be to your dad."

Those words were among the greatest gifts he could have given me. After he left, I contemplated our relationship. Shean had been in Las Vegas, witnessing how my dad and I had the best relationship of our lives during those years. I hadn't realized our son was absorbing all that.

During the last hours before getting released, my mind retraced the many steps in my life that had led me to that hospital bed. With each step, I have intended to accomplish something.

There have been so many times in my life when I've bowed my head and stated my intentions to God. I thought about how each step toward an intention is an act of free will.

But acceptance of the bigger plan also has to be part of it—thy will be done. I've had and accomplished many goals in my life, but I realized then that no step along the way was the destination. It was only movement. When I went to junior high, I learned what I needed to learn, but I didn't stay in junior high forever. Junior high was a step. Each time Laurrana and I had studied a spiritual tradition or learned martial arts, we took another step.

The problem with organized religions is that they define their box. It's fine to step inside the box and learn what they have to teach, but the leaders believe they are the only ones with the truth, and they want everyone else to believe it, too. Too many religions say, *We have something, and you don't. If you're not one of us, then you don't get our special truth.*

When I was cradled in God's palm, I felt how everyone is connected. There is no "me," only "we." There is no "us versus them," only "us." Oh, it can seem like some cliquish organizations are all about "we" because they create a community. But the way they define their group is exclusive and homogenized. Too many organizations want their members to be cloned followers. Their leaders are really all about "me" and they want the collective groups to conform. They want their little club to be distinct from everybody else outside the group. That's not the sort of "we" that honors the individual light of each member. That's just a collectivized form of "me."

It is fine to take part in a religion and learn from it. It's wonderful to be part of a community, as long as the community is about "we" in a broad sense of connection and love. But religion is a box. It is a step toward learning, just like any phase of learning in life is a step.

The step is not the destination.

Otherwise, we give our power to the step.

Every choice and phase of my life led to October 10, 2022. It was all part of polishing the diamond. There had been no mistakes, only experiences.

The tenth day - prayers

Richard

Around 6 p.m. on my tenth night in the hospital, my wife said, "You wouldn't believe how many people are praying for you."

"Wow, I never thought of that."

She showed me videos sent by extended family members. My cousin Sonserae, whom I had only met once, had orchestrated the videos. This effort provided a tremendous sense of support. We could feel the many prayers from the unknown relatives, including the many tribal members where Sonserae lives.

We had been planning to attend a powwow in North Carolina to meet my indigenous family but had to cancel due to my health. My sixth-great-grandmother was full-blooded indigenous and married into my father's Leigon line. Her tribe still lives in the area and has a powwow every year. We had recently been in touch, and I was looking forward to fostering a connection with an entire community of family I didn't know existed while growing up in Las Vegas.

They were disappointed that we couldn't make it, and they sent out a call for prayer. Throughout my hospital stay, many friends, colleagues, and family members called and sent gifts. They wanted to visit, but my wife discouraged them because I was on life support, and it was too early to know my situation.

These gestures let us know they cared, and they were a great comfort to Laurrana. Never underestimate how a card or a text can ease the burden of people in crisis.

During that time, one friend phoned to tell me, "Richard, every person throughout your entire life, every person whose life you ever touched, every person connected to your life has formed an unconscious connection of love. You are receiving all that right now."

I talked with our daughter that evening, and I felt how dearly she wanted to be with us. She was especially giving a lot of emotional support to Laurrana, but she was still having a hard time living halfway around the world. She didn't know if I would pull through, and I could feel her sadness through the phone. I reassured her that her love and prayers were enough. I *knew* her love was enough, that *she* was enough. My fondest wish is for her to know it, too.

These conversations with Laurrana and our daughter made me think about prayer, and I pondered the mechanics of how prayer might work. That night, I had what I can only call a vision. I believe dreams can bring powerful insights into the subconscious and provide a channel to receive wisdom. This, however, was even more vivid and profound than any dream in my life. Here is what I saw:

> *It's nighttime, and dark. I'm miles above the earth, and I look down to see the silhouette of earth. I turn around and see that the God Ocean is right behind me, the same infinite God Ocean that I was in when my spirit left my body.*
>
> *Beneath me, I also see hundreds of little streams or rivulets of red*

lights close to the earth flowing towards me and under me. They are like twinkling little LED bulbs flowing underneath me and upward into the God Ocean.

Then I realize those lights are all people! I can see them all around the horizon from all parts of the globe. I also understand that these streams of light represent everyone on earth with whom I've ever made a heart connection, even casual ones. People were not doing this in a conscious way; it was happening continuously. Our spirits were communicating heart-to-heart without our awareness. Intentional prayers added even more to the stream of love I already felt.

Love is healing me from all directions.

Next, I see a large, pulsating source of light around the world, sending a river of love to me. I instantly know it is coming from

*our daughter and her family. I
tell our daughter not to feel bad
because she did not need to be
there physically. I could feel
her love, and it was the same
as if she were standing next to
my bed, holding my hand. She
absolutely couldn't love me any
more than she already does. We
were connected, and I could feel
her love completely, like she was
hugging me with all of her heart.*

When I awoke, I no longer hoped or believed in the power of prayer. I had seen those prayers working in real time. I got to witness how they supplement God's love. Again, the message came to me that separation is an illusion, and oneness is real.

The Voice had one more message for me:

There is only One.
There can be only One.
Richard, I am the one, One.

I marveled at how all the words I could muster—wonderful, amazing, infinite, divine—

wouldn't even come close to describing what God is. It would be a grain of sand compared to the vastness I felt.

Richard Version 1's birthday

Richard

On the morning that I was scheduled to leave the hospital, Laurrana wished me a happy birthday. I had lived to see my next year.

After such a long ordeal, they were releasing me to go home. Shean and Laurrana helped me into a wheelchair and pushed me outside.

I felt the cool autumn air on my skin, the sun on my face, and the sense of immense gratitude for experiencing the outdoors. It felt like a lifetime since I had breathed fresh air. This was the first time since my near-death experience. It felt amazing to be alive again! There was a connection to nature that was extra precious now.

When I spotted our car, it hit me what a sense of humor God has. When paramedics had raced me through those hospital doors fourteen days earlier, I died. We could create an epitaph for Richard Version 1, who died on that day, but even more important than when the first Richard died, was that I would forever consider that day to be the birthday of the new me, Richard V2.

Now, I was doing the sequence in reverse—I was leaving through those same doors, returning home with my love, Laurrana. And this just *happened* to be my original earthly birthday, the day Richard V1 had taken the first breath of life in a hospital with my beloved mother.

God was laughing, "Do you see now? There are no coincidences."

Forsaken?

Laurrana

On the morning of Richard's birthday, Shean and I got busy decorating the house for his homecoming. I wish I could say that bringing Richard home in a wheelchair was a purely joyous occasion for me, because it should have been. This was a milestone he almost didn't live to see. I wasn't about to ruin it for everyone by expressing how distraught I felt.

Reality is often so much more complex than platitudes that say, "You should be happy right now. You should be grateful."

I was happier than I could express that Richard was still alive. *But for how long?* I was grateful,

98

but those "should" feelings only added weight to my already frazzled state of being. The truth was, I felt more like a mom going through a personal crisis on a child's birthday. Moms will make a party of it even if we are hurting. We do it because that is what the day calls for. We do it even though throwing a party requires even more energy—energy that has already been drained. We dig deep into a well that feels empty because that is what the day needs from us.

Birthday or not, homecoming or not, I was exhausted and completely overwhelmed inside. How on earth would I physically take care of him by myself? He had lost over thirty pounds and was so weak he couldn't even raise his arms, let alone walk. In the hospital, there is round-the-clock support. We pressed a button to get help transferring him from the bed to the wheelchair so he could go to the bathroom. Help arrived on rotation to clean his wounds and check his vitals. Staff brought meals and changed the linens. Sophisticated equipment monitored him nonstop, especially when I needed to step away for sleep or a shower. We didn't have any of that at home. How could they just wave us goodbye and good luck?

When they had released him to the rehab facility, he bled out partly because the staff were not trained at the same level as those in the hospital. I didn't even have as much training as the rehab staff, and I was only one person.

Yes, home healthcare would come, but that was only twice a week for an hour each visit. They would address the most critical needs, like dressing wounds. Yes, Shean would be there too, but he had to get back to work and had his own family.

The rest of Richard's care would fall to me. I'm petite and just one person. How would I possibly manage his physical necessities and also run our household by myself?

I knew well that he had a second bleed because they had not finished all the banding to fix all the varices. Nobody could honestly reassure me they had now caught every one.

I wanted answers, but the doctors could not say with confidence what I craved to hear: that everything was going to be okay. Their job was to relay the facts, and the facts were not reassuring in the slightest. They instructed me to be on the lookout because it could happen again at any time. We might go home today, and I might be planning his funeral tomorrow.

Now that he had survived two, I did not want him to die on my watch. He beat the odds twice, but three could be final. How much borrowed time were

we being given? A day? A year? Five years? That's a terrible feeling, the worst kind of anticipation.

Worse than the lack of comfort from Richard's doctors was that I was receiving no reassurance from the spirit. Why was the channel silent? I usually had strong spiritual impressions, like the day I knew to go to the hospital first. Yes, intellectually, I could tell myself that I was not alone spiritually, but I felt very alone.

Another layer that I couldn't admit aloud was that Richard was different. Of course, I felt happy for him that he'd had a marvelous spiritual experience. Anyone who conversed with him could tell he was completely blissed out, and I was in awe of all the love he radiated. His calm sense of peace and good humor through all his physical trials inspired me. I always knew Richard was an amazing soul and a born leader, and now I wanted to know what he was experiencing on a spiritual level.

We'd not had the time or privacy to talk about our feelings. I was used to processing everything with him, but I had to put his physical needs first right now. I was also accustomed to him helping me carry the weight of life, but I couldn't burden him with my troubles at the moment. And since he was reacting to everything with the glow of whatever he had seen, I worried that if I shared my struggles, he might respond with how great everything is on the other side. That was the last thing I wanted to hear when I pined for him to stay with me on this earth.

Our amazing son was right there with me, hanging a Happy Birthday banner. He would step up and do anything I asked. Our daughter provided immense support by phone since she was living overseas and couldn't return home to be with us in person. I knew I wasn't alone and felt ungrateful even thinking I was.

Yet, if I were honest, I wanted to cry out, *Why hast thou forsaken me?*

It reminded me of being a child when my mother was in the hospital with polio. Everyone was consumed with her care, and the dread of uncertainty hung over our family. Would she survive? Would she come home? Would she be wheelchair-bound for the rest of her life? What would our family look like in the aftermath? I was a skinny, little, frightened child then. I had been old enough to see and feel everything with a maturity far beyond my years, and yet I was totally alone in the emotional experience. There had been no one in my life to receive that little girl's grief and anguish, no one to reassure my fears.

The memory of that experience flooded my

senses, and I excused myself from Shean for a moment. I went into the bathroom to regain my composure. As I sat with those thoughts, the answer hit me all at once:

> *That's it! That's exactly what I need to remember—my mother's polio. I had been through that to prepare me for this now. That experience as a child gave me a window into what to do. I already know how to care for someone in a wheelchair. I already know how a family survives one of the worst circumstances. In the most trying of circumstances, I know how to come out on the other side. We are going to be okay. Richard was kept alive for an important reason, just like my mother had been. This is bigger than me.*

I understood I had not received direct comfort from the spirit for a short time because I needed to come to an answer on my own. It had not been a callous abandoning of me in my time of need. Nobody could do that work for me. A loving God would not deprive me of the knowledge I'd just received.

Figuring out this new guy

Richard

We arrived home to a big birthday banner and balloons. Laurrana and Shean then began reordering our home for my comfort. When Shean left us, I felt strong enough to sit up and converse. It was finally time for Laurrana and me to share our experiences.

I admitted to her, "I'm not the same man that you knew before I went to the hospital. I'm not the same man that you have been married to all these years and spent your life growing up with. Right now, I don't really know who Richard #2 is, but I do know I don't want to go back to being Richard #1."

I said it with a smile on my face and a twinkle in my eye. Then, while holding her hands and looking into her eyes, I said, "We will figure out this new guy together."

She nodded. "We've started a new journey."

She was listening intently, urging me to go on. I felt so much love toward her in that moment; she had always been so good at holding space for me.

I continued, "While I was out, God asked how I felt about all this. I said, 'I just feel love. That's all I feel, and I see it everywhere.' And then God asked, *What about everything else?*"

Laurrana studied my face as if she were seeing me for the first time. In a way, she was.

"I told God, Hey, I don't care about anything else. I'm in love with love, and I'm staying here." I said, gesturing toward my heart. I'm not going up here. I pointed to my head.

Laurrana wanted to know more about how I felt about being back in the material world.

"I was asked a question while I was out: 'Can you believe that God's hand is in everything?' And I said, 'Oh yeah, definitely.' Then God said, 'That's why you no longer care about the world, because you now see my hand in everything.'

A ground for the current

Laurrana

The night Richard came home, we finally had a chance to talk. I had been waiting until he felt strong enough, and we wanted privacy anyway. I had received an answer that comforted me with strength, but still no assurances about how much time we might have.

I tried not to feel wounded when he said he no longer cared about the world. I worried he might

105

become uninterested in life when I needed him to be invested in getting his health back. What if he became despondent and pulled away from me? I have heard of other people who have had near-death experiences, and they often have difficulty returning to the physical world. They don't want to be *here* when they know how good it feels to be *there.*

I was also envious that he had the luxury of not worrying. Sure, I was glad he didn't have that burden when he needed his strength, so I ended up worrying enough for both of us.

He took my hand and said, "What I mean is that all I care about is love. I can feel that in anything: the kiss of a butterfly, a smile for our grandchildren, and you. I love you."

"I love you too."

He continued. "You were the anchor that brought me back into this plane. It's like I had become electricity in the air, and you were a ground for the current, the path of least resistance that I grabbed hold of. You channeled me back here."

I worried he might resent coming back, but his eyes shone with gratitude. I could see that, and I felt at ease for now.

"Happy birthday, honey," I said, kissing him on his forehead.

I remembered the beam of light that connected us, reigniting his breath. I loved him beyond words.

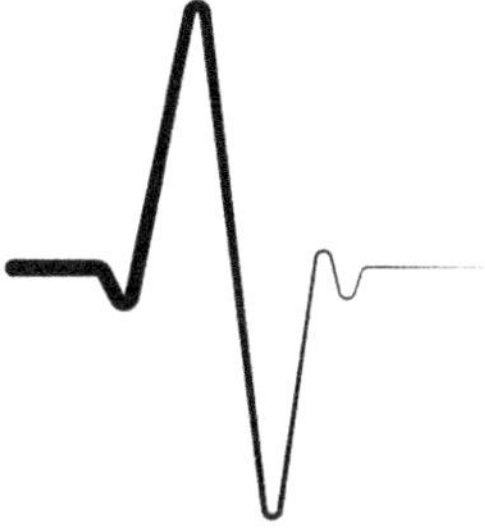

Chapter Five: Life After

"You must be glad you survived"

Richard

After coming home, we started getting visitors to wish me well. I felt a surge of love toward and from each of them.

I also found myself puzzled at how to respond when they said, "Boy, I bet you're glad to still be here." How could I tell them that, yes, I was a thousand percent on board with the divine plan of me being back, but I would have been happy to stay where I was.

It seemed like all I had to do was blink an eye, and I might have remained in that place. But I got sent back before anybody gave me that choice.

Instead of telling them all that, I described my experience like I was a child dancing to music. I could see flashes of recognition and hope on their faces. When I told them of God's hand in everything on this earth and how we are not being judged, they visibly brightened. I could see their worldly burdens lifting.

In turn, I felt grateful when they allowed me to share, because sharing had a profound effect on me, too. Forming words for what happened helped me call down the experience I'd had in spirit so it could cross over into this physical plane. Speaking required me to translate concepts and feelings—as well as I could— into language. My physical ears then heard those words, and my physical brain absorbed them. Speaking made the experience a tangible part of Richard's body.

Since my event, I no longer go into memories that evoke could have/should have/would have. I might see one or two, but there's no energy there. There's no judgment. When they drift up, a smile comes over me. It's as though those memories are posters with a big rubber stamp CANCELED across the front. I think often of the lesson I learned that first day when "The Voice" showed me unconditional, infinite acceptance and love.

My life had never been a series of events that were being monitored. I was not being judged, only loved and accepted by my creator.

In attempting to explain, I have struggled with a few words and phrases more than most. One was God. Maybe that was the best word, but it just seemed so small. I was also concerned because people react to the word God in so many ways based on their religion, beliefs, and prejudices. All that gets in the way. And to call God "Something" doesn't work, does it? So, how could I call God "Voice?" Or even, "Love?" God is all that and more. I feel more comfortable saying, "Divine Consciousness," or "Universal Consciousness." But I also worry that people will misunderstand that too. I realized I would just have to do my best.

I have also stumbled over the term "near-death experience." My death took me out of my body, "home," and then back to my body on earth. The way I see it, I died and was sent back, so it makes sense to call it a "death experience." I didn't "nearly" die. So, for a long time, I told people, "I died, and now I'm here."

I vividly remember talking to a healthcare professional on one of my visits.

When I told him I died and came back, he said, "No, you didn't."

We circled the subject, and his face grew redder and redder. I soon dropped it and instead asked Laurrana to bring him a cupcake. She had brought a box of them to share with all the hospital staff who had been so wonderful.

When we got home, I pondered why my story had touched a nerve in him. After doing a little research, I learned that in medical schools, students are taught that there is a clear line between life and death. Alive is alive, and dead is dead. Death is a permanent condition, and there are rules about when to record that a person has officially deceased. In the medical world, if you are breathing, you are alive. If you stop breathing, but then start up again, you did not die.

I have finally stopped being hung up on the terminology, accepting the term near-death experience or NDE. Sometimes I still call it "the event" or my "death event."

Richard's karma emptied

Laurrana

Friends know that prayer is part of my routine, not always in formal ways, but under my breath throughout the day. When they found out about Richard, they'd say, "You must have prayed for him to come back."

But I did not pray for that. It reminded me of when my mother was dying. She would say to me, "I am ready to go; I'm praying to go."

I wanted so badly to say, "Mom, I need you. Don't go."

But an inner voice whispered, Don't say anything to her. Don't you dare interfere.

After all, my mom had endured forty-six years in a wheelchair, with numerous medical issues. Who was I to attempt to place my own needs above hers?

I noticed another dynamic when people visited. I could tell they were interacting with the old Richard. They expected him to respond as he had done in the past. He still looked like the man they had always known, but he had changed. He had become a divine channel.

I told him, "It seems that when you died, all your karma from this life was wiped away. One life stopped, and another began on October 10."

He nodded and said, "Yeah, when I find myself trying to revert to old habits or thoughts, it's like those file drawers are empty."

It was a lot to unpack. A few days later, as Richard napped, I paused to take the same advice I'd given many caregivers. When I ministered to people in a hospice setting, I urged them to be mindful of self-care. I would share about the rejuvenating power of water, and how a shower or bath can make a world of difference to reset their energy. It even helps to step away for a few minutes to splash water on your face and let water from the faucet gently wash over your hands.

So, I indulged in a long shower, letting the cares of my mind untangle and my thoughts wander. A memory came to me from years earlier when an intuitively spiritual person told Richard that his life's purpose would be fully revealed later in life. In the coming decades, more than one person spontaneously made the same prediction. I realized we were now living in the moment they sensed would come.

Chapter Six: Regaining Health

The Lord's Prayer

Richard

The first months after my NDE were especially difficult on Laurrana. She put my needs before hers to make sure I was comfortable and healthy. She was exceptionally attentive, managing the regular household responsibilities, plus my share of the chores and the added burden of nursing me. She didn't complain, but she was exhausted from taking me to endless doctor's appointments, physical therapy, and nursing me to recovery.

We went to so many doctor's appointments that we had a running joke about all the hospital gowns I had worn, each with different prints and patterns. One time, I remember walking down a hospital corridor wearing one with fall colors.

I mimicked the walk of a runway model, "And this gown is from our fall collection." Laurrana followed close behind, giggling and trying to keep the back from flapping open.

Humor aside, she couldn't help but worry that we'd only be granted a temporary reprieve, and that my stint on earth might be up soon. Even if I lived a long time, we didn't know what that might look like. She was grieving the loss of our plans and dreams. Would we ever travel again? Would the rest of her life be fenced in by caregiving?

Laurrana would have some trauma to unpack when we were out of the worst danger. It took almost a year for her to get back on a regular gym schedule and start attending to her wounds.

Meanwhile, my doctors have continually been amazed at my recovery. There isn't a doctor who would have predicted where I am today. They credit a lot to my healthy lifestyle beforehand, making it so I only had to heal from the event and not prior abuse of my body. They say that liver damage is irreversible, but test results show that mine is healing itself.

When I went to see my liver doctor, he ran tests for the markers of cancer because that is usually where liver disease ends up. But after he got back all the lab work, he said, "Your numbers came in, and you're as healthy as I am. You and I have the same liver number."

When a friend asked why my body is healing so well, I said I believe it has to do with the breath of life and the Lord's Prayer.

People say that I look better than I have in years. When I look back on pictures of me during our Colorado phase, I think that guy looks like he has been beat up by life and isn't real excited about anything. I also think my health was worse than anyone realized for a long time, at least twenty years.

When people say I look younger now, it tracks the way I feel. I wake up each day knowing that God is love and love is everywhere. Therefore, love is God, and God is everywhere, and it's all the same. I have increased my awareness that every breath is divine.

I am the inhale; I am the breath. I am the exhale.

I also believe the Lord's Prayer has a lot to do with my recovery. It has always been a way for me to focus my energy on God, and it has become even more meaningful now. To me, The Lord's Prayer invokes respect, humility, and a request for Divine will to be done. It is a reminder to me to let go of all judgment.

A few months ago, my ten-year-old granddaughter asked a question that surprised me: "How do you feel about religion?"

I thought, I'd better be careful. Then I said, "Religion's okay, but you don't have to go into a church to talk to God. Each religion is like a box, and you can go to a church to gain knowledge and wisdom, but you don't have to be stuck inside that box. It's not a destination. It's like how I went to elementary school, and that school was a box. I learned what I needed to learn, but I didn't stay there forever."

She thought about my answer and said, "I agree."

Then I showed her a picture on the back of my phone of Mother Mary and Jesus so she could see that I have a relationship that has nothing to do with a particular church.

I always told our kids, "You need to take what we've taught you and figure out what works and what doesn't. I give you permission to follow your own path. Please do not carry on the part that doesn't work for you."

I'm sure I passed along stuff that wasn't helpful. They need to let go of that.

Thoughts on healthcare and NDEs

Laurrana

In the two years since Richard's experience, one of my self-care activities has been journaling. I have always been an active writer in this way, and my journals gave me a safe space to process emotions and also any insights that came through the journey. Here is an excerpt from a poem I sketched during this time, entitled "Perfection."

There's no such thing as perfection
I tried it and suddenly found
If I keep going in that direction
I'm probably going to drown
There's no such thing as perfection
Just reflection, retrospection,
embracing the now
While navigating my new
direction
And welcoming life's path
somehow.

Another topic I pondered in my journal was the state of medical care in this country. Here are some of those thoughts, which I sense are worth sharing here.

I appreciate the amazing advances in medicine that gave Richard such remarkable care. But there is still so much they don't know. We had been doing all the surveillance things, and they still didn't catch it in time.

Richard saw how the power of prayer and people's connection to spirit have an effect. These unquantifiable factors are left out of the scientific mindset. Richard's situation left a lot unexplained.

America has a sick-care plan, not a health plan. There are so many brilliant specialists, but they don't know what the others do. They don't want to step on each other's toes. They will say, "That's not my specialty, and I can't speak outside my expertise." Case in point: Richard's GI bleed happened in the esophagus, and yet it related to the liver. Everything in the body is connected, just as everything in the Universe is connected.

There are modalities out there that care for the whole of the being, but they're not supported by our insurance or medical community. So, those modalities haven't made the same advances.

Another topic that Richard and I have mulled over is how his experience is like or different from other NDEs. It has become clear that people receive the experience they are prepared for, and they may be visited by whatever beings of light will resonate most with their spirit. Richard had a relationship with Mother Mary, which is why she came to him.

Some people who die are not greeted by a divine messenger at all. There is no right or wrong ideology behind the symbols that are presented to one versus another. The details can vary. What matters is the common thread of light, acceptance, and love.

Another profound insight is that advances in medicine today have allowed more people to cross to the other side and be resuscitated. When these people come back, they bring profound messages to share. We believe these messages are of critical importance for our day. It is no coincidence that this is happening more now than ever before. Each person who returns from the other side brings back such a powerful resonance of light; they raise the vibration of the entire planet. This is exactly what is needed at this moment in history. People like Richard are providing a spiritual counterbalance to the conflict we are seeing in the world.

While it might seem like the field of NDE

stories is crowded, we believe that could never be the case. Each provides a unique witness, a unique testimony. The planet needs even more witnesses of God's love and light, not fewer.

Caregiving

Laurrana

For a full year, my days revolved around getting Richard's meds ready, helping him each day, and making sure he got the meals and sustenance he needed. There is so much to caregiving.

Occasionally, I confided in people about how overwhelmed I was. Too often, they responded in a patronizing tone, "You got him back. You should just be grateful."

I was, of course, but I knew they didn't get it.

Even though the workload of caregiving was physically demanding, I constantly muttered "thank you" prayers because I knew that his return had not been promised. I felt immense joy to have him back, and I still did not know how long we might have or what the future would bring. I never lost the memory of my heart breaking open that day in the hospital. Every day was a bonus day.

As I carried out my daily tasks, I thought of

the millions of people who are in their little houses doing the same thing every day. Nobody even knows about them. They never get a phone call, a hand on the shoulder, or a hug. I had far more support than they did.

That part touched me. I just wanted to go to every house I could and let those people know it was going to be okay.

I thought about what I had learned from my mother's polio experience, but also realized I still needed to let go of some programming that became part of me when my mother went into the hospital. While she was gone, I got shuttled between several environments each day: from a neighbor's home before school, then school, then in the care of some nuns, then with another neighbor, and finally with my father late in the evening.

I learned to navigate each environment, intuitively figuring out that each one had different expectations and needed different behaviors from me. To survive, I constantly did temperature checks to see whether the people responsible for me were okay. Were my actions and behaviors okay with them? It made me very attuned to other people's needs—at the expense of my own.

People of that era didn't believe it was

appropriate to ask children how they were coping with hardships. They underestimated how much children can understand, and they thought it best to shield us from hard experiences. They weren't shielding me from anything because I was already acutely aware of everything and understood far more than they imagined. How could they protect me from something that I was in the middle of living?

Because nobody talked to me, I had to carry the burdens by myself as a child. Instead of having an outlet to share my grief, I took on helping other people carry their burdens. As the eldest, I tended my younger siblings and even assisted the adults, too. I became the good daughter who helped and obeyed.

The takeaway for me is to temper self-sacrifice with self-love and self-care. Our light and physical energy are to be given, but also treasured. When we view physical energy as a valuable resource, we use it wisely, not squandering it in ways that are not valued.

Before this experience with Richard, I thought I had a handle on the imperative for self-care, but I learned I had some deep-seated patterns to break. I now realize I don't have to exhaust myself trying to understand other people, going to great lengths to make sure they feel understood. Other people don't always show up the way I show up. It's common to think that when we show up for someone, they will be the same way.

When they don't, I have realized I can either feel badly or let it go. I can decide that they are just being who they are, and they might not be able to give. For me, it was an act of self-care to let go of expectations. It's important not to lower our vibration to meet where other people are, and also not to expect them to move. If they decide to make a change, then that is their decision to make. Someone is just where they are, and that is as far as they can go right now. Sometimes this means allowing certain relationships to go. Just thank them, love them for who they are, and bless them. Then move on.

Some people are no longer allowed to walk through the door into my space. And I refuse to make myself smaller so other people can feel okay.

This phase of life made me even more grateful for Richard, who really is an amazing soul. I am also so grateful for our son, who has been physically and emotionally supportive, and our daughter, who checks in with me almost daily. She wishes she could be with us, but she and her husband live overseas with their young children and a career situation that made it impossible for them to visit during this time.

Our children are both generous givers, and

we are so proud of who they are. Others have been wonderful, too. There are more people to thank than would be possible on these pages, lest we inadvertently leave someone out.

Richard Version 2 brought something of a role reversal. In years past, I was often out of touch with my body, and Richard grounded me. He has so often brought me back into the 3-D world and made sure I was getting sustenance.

But he came home from the hospital pretty outside his body. He was lost in these other worlds, and I needed to be there for him as a grounding force. We both knew it. That's why I made sure to eat regular meals. I also drank lots of water so I could carry out the physical demands.

Finally, after about fourteen months, I could no longer ignore my health, so I walked into the gym again. I've always taken care of myself physically, and so I had been feeling out of sorts. There came a moment of realization that I could no longer afford to ignore what I needed. That doesn't take away from my desire to be of service to others; it's an imperative so I can continue to give.

When I finally made it through those doors, I came alive. I started working out, and I was part of the world again. I had lost a lot of muscle, but it felt great to gain a sense of normalcy there, reconnecting with the collective. I've been doing that most of my life, so being away from groups meant I wasn't getting the charge I am used to. So, the gym became my recharging station. I could go there, work out, and gain the energy I needed.

There were other internal aspects of self-care that I relied on whenever I had a few minutes to myself.

As he recovered, I had to learn when I was overcompensating, taking on more than necessary. Richard reminds me when I am overdoing it. I have learned something important:

Slowing down is a necessity for true progress.

Prayer is a nearly constant part of my life. I also began taking more downtime to write, process my thoughts in a journal, meditate, and especially be alone. I find that alone time is vital to sort things out, to feel autonomous, and to clear my head.

Here is an example of what I journaled about during this period:

Being in silence with myself, I haven't missed a thing. Instead, I've gained everything. Non-

> *resistance to what is, is the*
> *fastest way to healing. Naming it*
> *instead of blaming it allows me*
> *to evolve in a healthy way. I don't*
> *have to make somebody else*
> *wrong or be wrong myself. New*
> *choices have shown themselves,*
> *as old choices have dropped*
> *away. In divine perfection, my*
> *being is whole and evolving, no*
> *matter what it looks like.*

Feeling so alone during this time caused me to reach deep within and call up my courage to live a life authentically real for me, without outside influence. Standing there with nothing but my reflection, I learned how to choose myself while in crises, to recognize my own strength, to acknowledge my own resilience, and to honor my own needs.

Meanwhile, Richard rehabbed fast, doing everything ahead of schedule. He regained his abilities way ahead of the timeline. His diligence made it so much easier. My fears about him becoming despondent were unfounded. Yes, he was given a fatal diagnosis, so we take managing his health seriously each day. We are not about to squander the gift of time. But he doesn't let the diagnosis define who he is. Instead, Richard relates to his divine purpose.

What gets under your skin isn't real

Richard

I felt bad for Laurrana because I'm not the same person I was when we were in college. I look like the same guy, but I'm not. It's hard for her to have conversations with me about things that matter in life because they don't matter to me anymore.

One of the Ah-ha's I got in the hospital was that whatever gets under your skin—whether a minute ago, a week ago, or a year ago—isn't real. It doesn't matter. But did it take you out of your heart? If it did, then what are you doing?

Should I have done this or that? I'm not talking about morality; I'm talking about judgment. There is no judgment because love is all that matters. So-called mistakes do not matter. There are only choices. Where were you coming from when you made that choice? Were you coming from your heart? Intention is what matters. The world needs more unity, love, and encouragement. Not condemnation. God is love; God is not judgment.

Showing up

Laurrana

On a day recently, something happened that I want to share as an example of the kind of judgment people are carrying around, and how they need messages of unconditional love. I was standing in line at the grocery store with artichokes on the conveyor belt. The woman in front of me turned around, and when her eyes lifted to mine, she began to cry. She apologized and, in heavily accented English, leaned in and whispered that she was having a miscarriage right then.

I hugged her. At that moment, I felt such compassion for her that my eyes may have given it away. She looked at me as tears ran down her cheek and walked toward me. It felt natural to embrace her as a soothing gesture.

She responded, "Thank you; I needed to know I wasn't alone."

Once the cashier finished ringing us up, we stopped and talked for a while.

I retrieved my Miraculous Medal, which I always carry. It is a Catholic symbol associated with many healings and miracles, and I pressed it into her hand as a gift. I told her it is a symbol of love and healing.

She said, "I believe it."

It was not a religious gesture; it was from my heart as one mother to another. Her accent and the way she was dressed told me she was from another country, carrying different cultural beliefs, yet I felt prompted to give it to her. Although I was aware that her customs and traditions may not include an understanding of the significance of the Feast of the Miraculous Medal, it was gifted as a symbol of universal motherhood. She seemed to know that as she received the medal into her hand.

Then she asked in a pleading voice, "What am I doing wrong that caused this?"

I responded emphatically, "You didn't do anything wrong. This little soul isn't meant to come into the world right now. It will come later, so do not worry. It's not the right timing. This soul is in God's hands."

She thanked me as she wept, and she clutched the medallion to her heart.

That was not the first time I'd been with someone who was miscarrying. It strikes me that my professional calling has been to help people with the transitions around death. On occasion, that has meant being there to bear witness when an unborn body has not properly developed, and the soul attached to it is called to wait for another time. My role then is not to help the dying, but to comfort the mother left grieving the loss of what might have been.

On that day, this sweet woman was bearing the energetic weight of blame—that the miscarriage must have been her fault, that it was a kind of punishment. I felt her release all of that as we hugged.

I wish the whole world could release the ideologies that tell us we are constantly being judged. I wish everyone could feel the peace that Richard exudes. He radiates a knowledge that God's hand is in everything, not in a way to test or judge us, but only in love.

Yes, terrible things can happen to the best of people. My dear grandmother was murdered. She taught me so much about real charity and spirituality, yet God did not stop a murderer's free will from harming her. It was heartbreaking and brought trauma to my family.

Yet, I know evil will not ultimately win the day.

It is time for the old beliefs that no longer serve us to fall away. And the old constructs are crumbling around us. The planet is at an inflection point of tremendous change. The pain body has grown so big, and the collective appetite for more has become a monster. People who are undeveloped in their understanding violate others who get in their way. We are all feeling it, whether we realize it or not. We sense a tipping point.

The old ways don't work anymore, and as the old ways crumble, there is an existential threat to those who have dominated others and our earth for so long. They are unwilling to change, and that is why we are seeing a resurgence of ugliness. The ones who have hoarded power are doubling down on what they know.

What should spiritual people do? Yes, there is a time and a place to stand up, but doing so requires prudence. The worst thing would be to reduce our vibration, which serves no one.

We can elevate humanity by staying grounded in love and by nurturing each other. Remember what I said earlier about not trying to push the river? It feels to me like a great flood is raging right now. The destructive power of water is not to be underestimated. If you see a flood coming, do you fling yourself into the middle of the torrent? True, some people are called into active roles, while others will be called to take protective measures for what matters most. Regardless, we should all seek to see with our hearts and help others move to higher ground.

Chapter Seven: Travels

Indigenous connections

Richard

At various times in our lives, we have become connected to indigenous people. When we moved to Colorado, we were totally lost and didn't know what we would do. We moved to a town with one stoplight, and I got a job in an Ace hardware store running their electrical department, making six dollars and seventy cents per hour.

One day, I came home and there was a

group of Lakota grandmothers in a circle, including Laurrana. They were doing some kind of ceremony. I had never met any of them before. Somehow, she had met one of these women through a mutual friend, and she introduced Laurrana to more. After that, I would come home to a drum circle in our living room.

Soon, they were inviting us to their sweat lodge. They taught her to make various traditional handicrafts, and did the medicine wheel at Garden of the Gods. These women lived in the mountains, did intricate needlework, practiced indigenous medicine, and began teaching their ways to Laurrana. They embraced her as an adopted member, and even taught me how to tie my long hair into a Chongo, which is a traditional hairstyle worn by members of several tribes of the Southwestern United States.

Laurrana had a connection to them that went much deeper than mere friendship. Our association with them became very healing to us and was part of our journey of learning. They came out of nowhere and embraced us during a most difficult time of our lives.

Around that same time, we facilitated a sacred site tour to Chichén Itzá, Mexico. We were there to witness a ceremony on March 20 when the sun lines up on one of the Mayan temples. They had cordoned off an area with hazard tape to keep tourists away from the indigenous matriarchs who would perform the ceremony. Then, all of a sudden, three grandmothers ducked under the tape and took Laurrana by the hand. We did not even speak the same language, but they intuitively brought her into the circle. They gave her a rattle, smiled at her, and wouldn't let her leave until she danced with them. They just zeroed in on her out of the crowd.

Fast forward to 2022, when we had planned to attend the annual powwow held by the Occaneechi Band of the Saponi Nation with my indigenous relatives. We ended up having to cancel our trip when I had my death experience, and they prayed for me. Finally, by the fall of 2024, my health had returned enough so we could travel to North Carolina for it. Several of my tribal member cousins suggested I apply for official tribal membership, so they helped me fill out and submit the paperwork.

I had never met any of them in person, but they welcomed Laurrana and me fully into the family and treated it as a homecoming. Laurrana had done much of the genealogy, so she knew how people were related, and she was eager to visit the cemetery. They regaled us with family stories, and the love they showed us was unbelievable. They were not interested in separation, only reunion.

I grew up with one mom, one dad, one sister, and nobody else for three states away. All of a sudden, I was surrounded by people who were studying my features for resemblance to other family members and wanting to take pictures with me. It was a singular experience to walk on the farmland my family had settled, to meander country roads built upon old horse trails, and to feel the imprint of my people in that place. The whole energy of the experience felt divine. It was an amazing privilege to be living in 3-D so I could go there with my twin flame.

The gift of another Christmas

Richard

For Christmas of 2024, Shean arranged for all of us to fly overseas to be with our daughter and her family. We hadn't seen her family in person in three years, and I think the last time we were all together at Christmas was before our kids had kids. Shean was driven to bring his whole family back together in person.

I wasn't so sure I would feel up to it, but Shean just moved forward as if it would all work out. And it did. Laurrana bought her ticket early and said, "I'm definitely going." As the time neared, I got the green light from my doctors, and I also prayed and listened to my body to sense whether it would be safe for me to go. When I felt clear on all fronts, we bought my ticket. We couldn't have done it without Shean's vision and determination. Both of our children are the kind of people who make things happen.

So, Laurrana and I, Shean, his wife, and their child, and our daughter's family went sightseeing. What we enjoyed the most was just spending time—time we almost didn't have. We also cherished time with our grandchildren, so they can have stronger memories of us.

In reflecting on the time together, Laurrana said, "My grandparents' memories hold me up every day. Their light is such an important part of me, and I want that for our grandchildren."

When anyone loses somebody unexpectedly, a longing will inevitably come, "What I would give for just one more Christmas, or even one more ordinary day." That puts in perspective just how precious our time together was.

Our daughter hired a professional photographer, so we have a lot of beautiful photos to preserve these memories together. I remembered how some of my most cherished photos are of her as a little girl wearing my work boots or on her Big Wheel next to my motorcycle. When I got home from the jobsite each day, she would run to the door to greet me. When we first arrived, I felt a glimpse of that little girl running to the door. During these past years, we have remained close through video chats, but there is nothing quite like basking in each other's presence in person.

That was the gift Shean gave us all. Maybe we would have gone anyway if my event had not occurred, but would we have appreciated it in the same way? Life is so precious, and when I almost died, it showed our children just how short our time together in this plane of existence will be.

Shean's gift reminded me of how I once went into a store to buy a pair of Lucchese boots. The sales guy and I meandered through conversation.

He said, "I can't count how many times a widow or family member has come in to order a new pair of Luccheses. They wanted to put them on the deceased in his casket. They were going to bury him in a new pair of boots. I don't say anything, but I'm thinking, *I wish that guy in the casket had a chance to wear them before.*"

Making that trip meant enjoying one another while we still had the chance instead of wishing we had after it's too late.

Being there really touched her. She said,

"Thank you so much for coming and loving me."

I said what I believe she needed to hear on a soul-level, "Here's what we can do. We can pray together. Let's just hold hands and pray with each other, and for each other, forever."

Back where we started fifty years later

Laurrana

In June of 2025, our children and the grandchildren met us for a week in Maui to celebrate our fiftieth wedding anniversary. In the week leading up to our trip, Richard played love songs for me and left little notes around the house.

When we arrived, we gave everyone leis made of Kukui nuts, which are a symbol of strong bonds between people. In old times, islanders burned the nuts like candles. On a deeper level, these leis are given to people who are bringers of light, which is how we feel about each member of our family.

Our kids arranged for our group to stay at an all-inclusive resort where the grandchildren enjoyed pools with water slides, and the two of us didn't have to worry about a thing. When we wanted to eat, we ate. When we wanted to play with the kids, we did. We basked in the sun and let the ocean's healing waters wash over and through us. Throughout our whole trip, we felt the warm, welcoming spirit of aloha everywhere. That gracious, relaxed mood permeated our souls.

On the afternoon of our actual anniversary, we all gathered on the beach in honor of the time and place where we married fifty years earlier. We renewed our vows in the presence of the people dearest to us, enveloped by their love and support.

While Richard had been in the hospital, I contemplated being a widow, walking through our empty house, and longing for the simplest of daily rituals. I knew that big holidays and anniversaries would be especially difficult in his absence. During our trip in Hawaii, there wasn't an hour when I didn't think of our immense good fortune to be there.

Our fiftieth wedding anniversary almost didn't happen. If Richard hadn't come back, maybe our kids would have planned the trip anyway to cheer us all up and remember him. He did come back, though. What a treat it was to enjoy him instead of only remembering him. We all basked in each other's company, laughing and talking. We could love each other in the here and now.

One afternoon, as Richard and I lay side-by-side in the sand, I noticed the two of us breathing in and out, naturally in sync. Each time an ocean wave crashed onto shore and retreated, it sounded like Mother Earth herself breathing with us.

I thought of Richard describing how each of us will eventually return to the vast ocean of love. We will be like raindrops dissolving into the whole. That thought gave me peace, knowing that even when death comes, we will never be far apart.

The breath is already in us, and we are already in the breath. We are never separate from the God Ocean of love. The end of our mortal time will not make that love any more real than it already is, only more immediate. Any sadness or hardship in this life will be but a moment, especially if we embrace the all-encompassing love that is endless in all directions, yet more subtle than a butterfly's kiss.

Epilogue: Thoughts for Our Day

Why was I sent back?

Richard

I've had people ask if I know why I was sent back. Richard Version 1 would have had a quick answer for that. Now? I don't know. I just remember the infinite ocean of energy and find it hard to drill down to such a finite question. All I know is "Thy will be done."

I understand that if anything's going to mess up, it will be my conscious mind, not my infinite mind. It wants to help, but if it gets overzealous, I'd just have to untangle it again. So for now, I'm so in love with love that I have no clue. That's probably where we should park it, so it doesn't get in the way.

What happens to personalities after death?

Laurrana

While we were working on this book, we had a dinner conversation with a friend who asked, "What do you think happens to people's personalities after we die?"

Here is my perspective, gleaned from a lifetime of intuitive gifts in which I have felt very connected to the other side, as well as what Richard brought back from his experience.

Once our loved ones cross over to the other side, their personality and challenges are no longer a part of who they are. While in body and on this earth, our loved ones had to deal with their own difficulties, and it took a toll. They may have had the best intentions, but hardships may have been in the way of fully expressing their love. After death, however, they become pure essence, and the soul can express its true nature effortlessly. They are free from the obstacles they faced in mortality, and they can clearly express love and offer support.

In my hospice work, I have seen countless examples of people who notice that following the death of someone they were close to, their life improved in unexpected ways. They receive help from the other side.

If you lose someone, I encourage you to pay attention to changes that occur after they are gone. Even amid deep grief, you may feel a sudden surge of newfound energy, and your life may feel easier. This is a palpable way our loved ones can let us know they are still with us.

I have seen this happen even when people had tumultuous relationships in life. This has taught me that there is always room for grace and forgiveness. Each person lives in a way they are capable of at the time. We may carry grief in our hearts for what could have been. We may regret that we might have done things differently.

However, you deserve grace, too. You face challenges that interfere with your ability to fully embrace the depths of your love. Do not despair. It is my fond hope that my husband's story will help you feel loved and free from judgment. Do not be hard on yourself, but practice doing the best you can for now. Remember, there is always room for grace!

Messages for turbulent times

Richard and Laurrana

We are living in a turbulent time, but we must not give in to fear. We must trust that turbulence is to be expected as the world is being prepared for transformation into a higher plane. Some people sense the old ways crumbling, and they will fight to keep everything as it was in the past. They are afraid of surrendering to love, afraid to lose their perceived sovereignty. They do not realize they are already one with all that is. Separation is an illusion. God has not given up on humanity, just as God never gives up on any of us.

It is up to us to open the door to our hearts and allow ourselves to feel love. When we do, we become a conduit for love and to accept our oneness.

Love is how we experience God in our lives. It is how we feel connected to God in our body, heart, and soul. When we allow love in, we allow God in. Love is an anchor to the collective. It is flowing around us at all times. All we have to do is open ourselves to it. When we do, we move the collective into a higher frequency of love on earth as it is in heaven.

You might think love is a subtle force, but it is the most boundless and powerful force there is or ever will be. How can anything be so subtle and yet so powerful? When we allow love into our hearts, we give it physical form, bringing it into this plane. This is what the world needs most at this moment in history.

With every breath, we give the Divine a physical ground on this plane. God is one with us in each breath we take. With each breath, we can let our awareness expand.

I am the breath (inhale).
I am the breath (exhale).

You are breathing as you read this, and we hope that from these pages, you can understand that there is something beautiful happening with every breath that you take. For a moment, just imagine all that is beautiful on this earth and inhale. Are you smiling? You're not smiling alone.

We are each like a drop of water that touches the ocean—instantly part of the whole ocean. There is no beginning and no end to that drop of water. We may think we are alone sometimes, but we never are.

Now is the time to allow ourselves to feel what touches our hearts. We can choose to engage with our Source in a dance, co-creating what is to come.

Each time we allow ourselves to give and receive love, we touch the ocean. It doesn't matter how big or small an act of love is. Perhaps it is a simple gesture of kindness or an encouraging word. We can lean into one another, strengthening someone else in the storm, and in turn, strengthening ourselves. That which we allow to touch our hearts, touches all.

Be the star that you are. Turn down the noise and align your mind with your heart. Working in harmony, let your light shine, illuminating the way for others.

Dedications

From Richard, this book is dedicated to:

My wife, children, and sister, who experienced a sudden loss, extreme uncertainty, and trauma through my death and subsequent illness. You lost—and regained—a husband, father, and brother.

To the first responders: 9-1-1 Dispatcher and Clark County Fire Department Rescue Unit R34.

To the E.R. and Critical Care team at St. Rose Dominican Hospital - San Martin Campus, and all the competent doctors, nurses, and staff members involved in my emergency and critical care.

To the competent post-hospital team of

doctors, nurses, and Spring Valley Hospital Medical Center staff members who were involved in my three-year recovery process.

Thank you!

Also, to the life partners and close family members who, unexpectedly, without notice or planning, find themselves without a spouse, husband, wife, mother, father, sister, brother, and then are overjoyed with their return. You live your trauma memories every day, knowing that if this happened once, it could easily happen again.

And foremost…

To Mother Mary. I humbly bow for having received your grace.

From Laurrana:

As the time drew near to publish this book, I felt the love and support of my ancestors, and I must acknowledge all who have gone before me, who held me up along with my Creator. My grandparents have been especially powerful influences, walking with me through every trial, challenge, and joyful experience: Aznive, Simon (Sam), Ursie, and Evo. They have made the gift of my life possible. Also, to my parents, Jack and Maryann, whose steadfast faith, endurance, and strong spirit gave me the ability to live a successful and spiritually fulfilling life.

Comfort Came, a Poem

To Richard from Laurrana

I watched you die, and comfort came to visit me

The infinite was with us

An unspoken calm filled the room

In the midst of life-changing crisis, serenity
covered us in its protective cloak

And at that moment, I knew you were taken care of

I recognized the safety of your soul's
fate, and all I knew was love

Trusting you were held in God's
palm and infinite wisdom

As light beamed from my heart to yours

White light

As grace claimed me for itself, love was everywhere

As you took a breath, you came back to me

And as I watched the breath breathe you

I exhaled in recognition

You hadn't left me after all

In awe, I smiled from the inside

Emanating out of you, aliveness returned

The impossible made possible

Miracles happen

Love prevails—You are love

It knows no bounds

Our union was not broken

As it continues on

Each precious day with you renews my faith,
reigniting the fire within that carries my love for you

About the Authors

Richard Leigon

Richard Leigon earned a degree in humanistic psychology from Sonoma State University. It was an emerging field at the time, and the subject matter lit his fire. After graduation, he sidestepped the California scene of the late sixties and was welcomed into a yoga ashram in Hawaii. There, he practiced meditation, yoga, and martial arts, which remained part of his life in the coming decades. Richard's career ultimately took a practical turn when he followed in his father's footsteps as a union electrician. An unexpected opportunity ultimately brought him back to his hometown of Las Vegas, where he served as Executive Director IBEW/ NECA – LMCC on a street named Leigon Way in honor of his father. Today, Richard is retired and enjoys his life as a grandfather.

Laurrana Leigon

Laurrana met Richard while pursuing her degree in Sociology at Sonoma State University. After recognizing their love, she joined him in Hawaii, where they married. Her thirty-year career as a hospice bereavement and comfort care coordinator prepared her in profound ways for Richard's death and return. She is a well-respected pioneer and leader in that field, which was new at the time she started. Laurrana helped create effective programs for hospice organizations that are still in use today. An avid reader and lifelong journaler, Laurrana pursued her passion for writing in retirement, starting with her grandmother's story. However, that project had to wait when Richard's experience plunged her into the role of full-time caregiver. After emerging from that ordeal, she felt prompted to turn their energy to this story.

###

Richard and Laurrana make their home in Richard's hometown of Las Vegas, Nevada, near their son and his family. They enjoy weekly video chats with their daughter and her family, who live abroad.

Connect with them at https://one-breath-nde.com

Book Club Questions

1. After you finished the book, what image or idea stayed with you the most?

2. One of Richard's great takeaways is that there is no judgment, only experiences and only love. How is this similar to or different from what you were raised to believe? What do you think about judgment at this point in your life?

3.   Have you read other near-death experiences? If so, how is this story similar to or different from those? What do you make of those differences?

4.   Mother Mary appears twice in Richard's life, first at the foot of his childhood bed, and then in the emergency room calling him back to life. Richard reflects that people receive the messenger they are most prepared to receive. How does this align with your beliefs or do you have a different view?

5.   Richard says that before October 10, 2022, he had *hopes and beliefs*, but afterward he *knew*. Is there a meaningful difference between belief and knowing? Have you ever had the experience of *knowing* something?

6.   How did Laurrana's perspective of grief and the weight of caregiving while Richard was "blissed out" affect you?

7.   Laurrana's thirty years of hospice work prepared her to let Richard go if it was his time. Have you ever been in a similar situation, or can you imagine you might react in her shoes?

8.   Richard and Laurrana deliberately stepped away from organized religion while maintaining deep, evolving spiritual lives. Richard uses the metaphor of religion as a "box" and a step toward learning, but not the destination. Do you agree or disagree? Where does that idea sit with your own faith experience?

9.   Richard described a God Ocean as a place of unconditional acceptance and infinite love. Does his description align with or challenge your own beliefs about what happens after death?

10.   Richard saw the power of connection and prayer like tiny rivulets of light coming toward him. What are your beliefs about prayer?

11.   Richard had an ongoing conversation with "The Voice" throughout his life. Could you relate to this, or was this part of his story foreign to you?

12.   When Laurrana brought Richard home from the hospital, she performed his homecoming while feeling completely overwhelmed inside, like a mother throwing a birthday party while in crisis. Have you ever had to hold it together for someone else while carrying your own burdens?

13.   Richard and Laurrana were always deeply spiritual and intuitive people. How do you interpret moments like Richard's motorcycle experience as a young man or when Laurrana's knees buckled and she dropped to the ground just before she learned her grandmother was murdered? What other examples from the book come to mind?

14.   Laurrana said she and Richard

have learned not to resist when energy isn't flowing, despite our culture pushing the idea of "you can do it" and "fight no matter what." What is your take on this?

15. One thematic element of the book relates to "twin flames," where two people are not only compatible, but who share a common mission and seem like two halves of the same whole. How does this differ from the idea of soul mates, or is it the same thing? Have you experienced this or known a couple you would describe this way?

16. Both Richard and Laurrana felt connected to their ancestors throughout their lives. Do you think ancestors remain in people's lives, either through memory, a DNA connection, or through a spiritual connection?

17. Richard reconnected with his indigenous family late in life, which was made possible by his survival. What did that thread in the story stir in you?

18.	The book explains the power of breath, where each inhale and exhale is a physical connection to the divine. What are your thoughts about breath? Has the book changed anything about paying attention in your life?

19.	If you could ask Richard or Laurrana one question that the book didn't answer, what would it be?

Photos

Laurrana's graduation - Laurrana's grandmother
Aznive, Laurrana, grandfather Evo, grandmother Ursie

Richard College Graduation - Mother Evelyn, Richard,
Father Ralph

Richard and Laurrana in 1998

Richard in their home in Colorado

Chief Golden Light Eagle, Laurrana, Bearcloud and Richard

Mother Mary

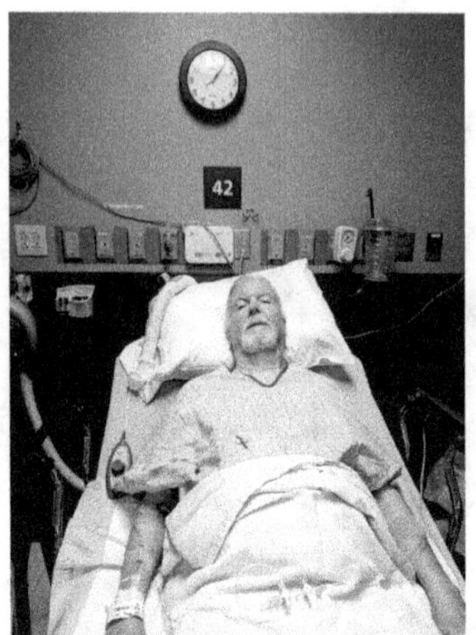

Richard in the hospital

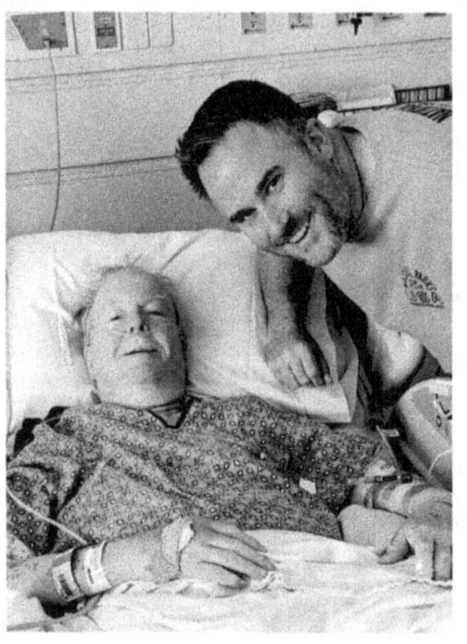

Son Shean in the hospital with Richard

Richard and Laurrana at Stonehenge

Son, Laurrana, Richard, and Daughter.

Richard, Laurrana, and Dr. Ares

*Richard five months after being released from the
hospital*

Linda Jeffries, Richard, and Sonserae Toles at the pow-wow

Richard and Laurrana renewing their vows

*The whole family together celebrating the fiftieth
wedding anniversary*

Richard and Laurrana renewing their vows

Richard and Laurrana Leigon